section 1: believe intro • Page 2

section 2: believe Jesus • Page 30

section 3: believe Peter • Page 38

section 4: believe Paul • Page 41

section 5: believe John • Page 49

section 6: believe Jude • Page 55

section 7: believe Matthew • Page 67

section 8: choose • Page 150

"It is not
WHAT WE DO
that determines
WHO WE ARE. It is
WHO WE ARE
that determines
WHAT WE DO."
- Neil T. Anderson

ricky russ jr • www.ChooseBelieve.com

tone

It's imperative that you know my tone in this book before turning the page.

Please know,
I'm not angry.
I'm passionate :)
I'm passionate about truth.
I'm passionate about believe.
I'm passionate about ignoring lies.
I'm passionate about showing others
what God showed me.

On November 23, 2014, God showed me something on a 5-hour flight from Charlotte, NC to Portland, OR that changed how I hear and see today. Here's the crazy part; what He showed me has always been there!

If at the end of this book you don't
choose believe,
that's your choice.

God said you are a:
saint (not a sinner saved by grace!) • Ephesians 1

belief

Why don't most believers believe in the power of belief? Jesus marveled at belief.

Why do lies seem to get more air-time than truth? Maybe people choose lies because they haven't seen the truth.

The good news is this; once you clearly see the truth, you can't help but see the lies in other things.

choose to believe!
choose believe

God said you are His:
possession • Genesis 17:8 & 1 Cor 6:20

who

*This book is for the follower of Jesus who knows deep down that something is still missing even though they are clean and sober.

*This book is for the follower of Jesus who wants to be clean and sober but doesn't believe in programs and steps.

*This book is for people who have yet to hear about their true identity.

*This book is NOT for someone who doesn't love Jesus and follows His teachings. Then again, maybe it could be.

> "An island of people who only KNOW about pennies and nickels can't be blamed for doubting
> the man who talks about his bag of quarters!"
> - unknown

God said you are His:
child • John 1:12

cobra effect

The term cobra effect originated in an anecdote set at the time of British rule of colonial India.

The British government was concerned about the number of venomous cobra snakes in Delhi.

The government therefore offered bounty for every dead cobra. Initially this was a successful strategy as large numbers of snakes were killed for the reward.

Eventually, however, enterprising people began to breed cobras for the income.

When the government became aware of this, the reward program was scrapped, causing the cobra breeders to set the now-worthless snakes free.

As a result, the wild cobra population further increased. The apparent solution for the problem made the situation even worse.

God said you are His: workmanship • Eph 2:10

selfness

What's the difference between selfness and selfish?

Selfness:
The state, quality, or condition of self.

Selfish:
Concerned only with oneself.

God said you are His: friend • James 2:23

i.den.ti.ty
noun:

1. the condition of being oneself and not another

Here's something I discovered:

A byproduct of identity = Purpose

A byproduct of purpose = Passion

A byproduct of passion = Sobriety

God said you are His: temple • 1 Cor 3:16 & 6:16

lie

The world says:

- You will pay for what you've done
- You are addicted
- You should take it one day at a time
- You have a disease
- You were born this way
- You're a sinner saved by grace
- You need to ask for forgiveness daily
- You're broken
- You're demon possessed
- You've messed up too much
- You need to work harder
- You're in bondage
- You need to attend another group
- You don't have enough
- You must first forgive yourself
- You are single, isolated, and alone
- You need to find a mentor

God said **you are** His:
co-laborer • 1 Timothy 5:18

believe

God said you HAVE BEEN:

- redeemed by the blood • Rev 5:9
- set free from sin /condemnation • Rom 8:1-2
- set free from Satan's control • Col 1:13
- set free from Satan's kingdom • Eph 2
- chosen before foundation of world • Eph 1:4
- predestined to be like Jesus • Eph 1:11
- forgiven of all your trespasses • Col 2:13
- washed in the blood of the Lamb • Rev 1:5
- given a sound mind • 2 Timothy 1:7
- given the Holy Spirit • 2 Cor 1:22
- adopted into God's family • Romans 8:15
- justified freely by his grace • Romans 3:24
- given all things pertaining to life • 2 Pet 1:3
- given great and precious promises • 2 Pet 1:4
- given ministry of reconciliation • 2 Cor 1:22
- access to God • Eph 3:12
- given wisdom • Eph 1:8

God said you are His:
vessel • 2 Timothy 2:2

sidecar

If you choose to ride in the sidecar on the motorcycle of life, you still get an exhilarating experience, but your environment, journey, and destination are dependant on the motorcycle.

Listen for God's voice in everything you do, everywhere you go; He's the one who will keep you on track.

God said you are His: witness • Acts 1:8

journey

definition: an act of traveling from one place to another.

For too long I've heard it said, *"Recovery is a Journey not a Destination."*

I disagree. I believe Recovery IS a destination. It's more than possible to arrive at this destination, celebrate it for a minute, and then move on to all that God has for you!

It's deception and unbelief that keep people on a journey traveling towards something they already have.

God said you are His:
soldier • 2 Timothy 2:3

in common

What do YOU think the words in the list below have in common?

12 steps, 8 principles, coins, clean days, sobriety, dry, AA, NA, SA, CR, broken, meetings, groups, sponsor, hurts, habits, hang-ups, recovery, and programs.

Something to believe:
As for you, the anointing [the special gift, the preparation] which you received from Him remains [permanently] in you, and you have no need for anyone to teach you. But just as His anointing teaches you [giving you insight through the presence of the Holy Spirit] about all things, and is *true and is not a lie*, and just as His anointing has taught you, you must remain in Him [being rooted in Him, knit to Him]. • 1st John 2:27

God said you are His:
ambassador • 2 Cor 5:20

serenity

definition: the state of BEING calm, peaceful, and untroubled.

The key word in this definition is BEING.

The serenity prayer: "God grant me the serenity to accept the things I cannot change; courage to change the things I can; and wisdom to know the difference."

Accept, cannot change, and change are action words (DO words), not BE words.

The Serenity Prayer was written by a theologian (Reinhold Niebuhr • 1892–1971).

If you claim to be a follower of Jesus, why not pray a prayer that Jesus prayed?

God said you are His:
building • 1 Cor 3:9

don't need

Believers don't need to "keep coming back".
Believers don't need "a group for that".
Believers don't need "a program".
Believers don't need "12 steps".

Is the goal of recovery to have 85% of people who go through "the program" to stay with the church and for nearly half to serve as church volunteers? In my opinion, that's not worth celebrating.

It's not church attendance and volunteering that keep people clean and sober.

It's not church attendance and volunteering that we are to seek first. But, if it was, what about the other six days of the week?

Believers need belief.

God said you are His:
husbandry • 1 Cor 3:9

documented

What's the difference between sobriety and documented sobriety?

They say, "Programs are a well-documented way for individuals struggling with sobriety to get the help they need from friends and family members to stay on track. A strong social support system can encourage growth and sobriety over time, whereas without a support group, and individual may fall back into addiction during difficult times."

In order to BELIEVE something, you must first choose not to BELIEVE what others BELIEVE when they tell you something that contradicts what Jesus told you to BELIEVE.

God said you are His:
minister/instrument • Acts 26:16 & 1 Tim 4:6

etc epidemic

The United States is NOT in the
midst of an opioid overdose epidemic.
Opioids are NOT killing people.
We don't have a heroin epidemic.
Etc.

"What we've got here is"
a Silent Epidemic of Identity Deficiency.

People perish for lack of knowledge.
People perish for unbelief.

Christians who believe in WHO
they are in Christ, don't and won't
abuse drugs, alcohol, women, children,
Etc.

God said you are His:
chosen • Eph 1:4

unbelief

Those who are TRUE followers of Jesus are NOT powerless against anything.

{ This resurrection life you received from God is not a timid, grave-tending life. It's adventurously expectant, greeting God with a childlike "What's next, Papa?" God's Spirit touches our spirits and confirms who we really are. We know who He is, and we know who we are: Father and children.

And we know we are going to get what's coming to us—an *unbelievable inheritance*! We go through exactly what Christ goes through. If we go through the hard times with Him, then we're certainly going to go through the good times with him! }
- The Message

God said you are His:
beloved • Romans 1:7 & 2 Thess 2:13

be-attitudes

The word "beatitudes" is not in the scriptures. Jesus never used this word.

This word was not even put into the Bible (as a headline) until the 1500s.

Go back and re-read the end of Matthew chapter 4 and all of 5 (not just verses 5:3-10).

If you have eyes to see, you might just walk away seeing how this section of scripture has been high-jacked and applied to fit a man-made formula!

There is so much more to this section of scripture than just 8 principles!

God said you can:
tread Satan under foot • Rom 16:20

problem

I've heard many people say,
"We can't love or pray the drug problem away."

That comment comes from a dark place of unbelief.

Jesus opens our ears (were deaf), and points things out to us (were blind) as we walk (were lame) with Him and talk (were mute) with Him. We are now sons (were poor) living (were dead) a new life with Him. See Page 89 • 11:5

Belief hears!
Belief sees!
Belief walks!
Belief talks!
Belief is free!
Belief lives!

The problem isn't the problem.
The problem is unbelief.

God said you can:
find mercy and grace to help • Heb 4:16

one step

Do you believe the "one step"
Jesus took in Mark 5 is possible for today?
Do you believe it was just for that time?
Do you believe Legion was a one-off?
Do you believe this "one step" occurred
only because it was Jesus?

Scripture says, Their herdsmen ran away and reported it in the city and in the country. And the people came to see what it was that had happened. They came to Jesus and observed the man who had been demon-possessed sitting down, clothed and in his right mind, the very man who had had the "legion"; and they became frightened.

Jesus didn't tell Legion to seek recovery. Actually, He did the complete opposite. Jesus focused on today, not on the past days that Legion spent in the tombs.

God said you can:
come boldly to the throne of grace • Heb 4:16

focus

We tend to see
what we're prepared to see.

A person's focal point causes them
to see Hurts, Habits, & Hang-ups.

It's possible to go weeks at a time on
a steady diet of selflessness without
focusing on Hurts, Habits, and Hang-ups.

Jesus said, "if anyone wishes to come
after Me, he must deny himself, and
take up his cross and follow Me."

When you turn your eyes upon Jesus
and His instructions; Hurts, Habits, and
Hang-ups grow strangely dim!

God said you can:
quench all the flaming darts • Eph 6:16

hell & jail

There's a thief in jail.
There's a thief in church.
There's a thief in hell.
There's a thief in heaven.

There's a sober person in hell.
There's a sober person in jail.

There's a drunk in heaven.
There's a drunk in church.

Your belief determines
your destination.

Don't look for verses to fit
your program, let the verses
form your thoughts.

God said you can:
tread on the serpent • Luke 10:19

time to drink

When it comes to sobriety, what do you do with Proverbs 31:6-7?

Give strong drink to him who is perishing, and wine to him whose life is bitter. Let him drink and forget his poverty and remember his trouble no more.

So, maybe he who is perishing needs belief, truth, and knowledge more than he needs sobriety. Because if he truly begins to believe, guess what happens?

God said you can:
declare liberty to captives • Isaiah 61:1

beLIEve

Choose to believe.
Don't listen to the lie.

Jesus said,
"the sheep follow Him because they know his voice. A stranger they simply will not follow, but will flee from him, because they do not know the voice of strangers."

This means a true believer hear voices every day. There are times when the stranger sounds like a well-meaning friend. There are times when the stranger sounds like a well-respected person.

Luckily, you get to choose
which voice you want to believe.

God said you can:
pray always and everywhere • Luke 21:36

meetings

Christians don't need meetings. I didn't say meetings are evil. I didn't say Christians shouldn't go to meetings. What I'm saying is if Christians believe they need meetings (meaning: they can't go without them), that's a prØblem.

If you hear a Christian say "meetings" more times than you hear him say "Jesus", that's a prØblem.

If you sit in a circle of 20 people who verbalize negativity, fear, and lies for two hours, your positivity, faith, and belief will erode. If you leave the meeting with less belief than when you walked into the meting, that's a prØblem.

It's not meetings that saves people's lives. It's belief that saves people's lives.

God said you can:
chase a thousand • Joshua 23:10

plan b

God is love. He still loves us even when we disobey. Just like He did with Adam & Eve. God's plan was for Adam & Eve to be naked in the garden, but they disobeyed and shame was born.

So, what does Love make? Clothes. God made Adam & Eve clothes. Clothes were plan b.

If we choose not to believe and instead choose "steps", He still loves us. He will still work all things together for good. But God wants us to believe. Jesus marveled at belief.

God said you can:
defeat (overcome) the enemy • Rev 12:11

52 weeks

Let's say
1 individual attends
1 meeting per week which lasts
2 hours, and their total commute
time adds up to
1 hour.

At the end of just
1 year, they will have given over
156 hours to meetings.
156 hours!

There are people who earn their
Bachelor's degree in less time than that.

1 year. Dedicate the next 52 weeks to the
1 step of believe and your life will change!

God said you can:
do all things through Christ • Philp 4:13

believe ricky?

Everything I've written to this point might sound extreme. You might be thinking, "This guy doesn't know what he's talking about." or "Well, obviously Ricky hasn't been through the kind of things I've been through." or "You can't apply 'believe' to everything."

At the time of writing this book, I have over 4,300 days of sobriety (alcohol) and 6,500 clean days (drugs). I've never had a sponsor, attended a group, or been to a meeting.

Other facts about me:
DUI: 2006 • PCS/DCS: 2000 • Aggravated Theft: 1995
Arrested: 5 times • Jail: 3 times • Probation: 2 times
College: No • GED: No • High School: 11th grade

I live a life of believe.

Still not convinced in the power of believe?

God said you are:
kept from falling • Jude 1:24

believe neil?

In the book *Who I Am In Christ,* Neil T. Anderson said,

"How we formerly identified ourselves no longer applies. When asked to describe themselves, people usually mention race, religion, cultural background or social distinctions. But Paul said none of those apply anymore, because our identity is no longer determined by our physical heritage, social standing or racial distinctions. Our identity lies in the fact that we are all children of God and we are in Christ. Although I am thankful for my physical heritage, I am far more grateful for my spiritual heritage. The practical significance of this essential truth cannot be overstated. A Christian gains forgiveness, receives the Holy Spirit, puts on a new nature and gets to go to heaven. A Christian, in terms of his or her deepest identity, is also a saint, a child born of God, a divine masterpiece, a child of light, a citizen of heaven."

Still not convinced in the power of believe?

God said you are:
complete in Christ • Colossians 2:10

believe jesus!

Jesus used the word "believe" over 90 times in the Gospels. I marvel at this!

1. Go; let it be done for you as you have **believed**.
2. Do you **believe** that I am able to do this?
3. but whoever causes one of these little ones who **believe** in me to sin,
4. For John came to you in the way of righteousness, and you did not **believe** him, but the tax collectors and the prostitutes **believed** him. And even when you saw it, you did not afterward change your minds and **believe** him.
5. Then if anyone says to you, 'Look, here is the Christ!' or 'There he is!' do not **believe** it.
6. If they say, 'Look, he is in the inner rooms,' do not **believe** it.
7. The time is fulfilled, and the kingdom of God is at hand; repent and **believe** in the gospel.

God said you cannot:
be separated from His love • Rom 8:35-39

8. Do not fear, only *believe*.
9. If you can'! All things are possible for one who *believes*.
10. Whoever causes one of these little ones who *believe* in me to sin,
11. Be taken up and thrown into the sea,' and does not doubt in his heart, but *believes* that what he says will come to pass,
12. Therefore I tell you, whatever you ask in prayer, *believe* that you have received it, and it will be yours.
13. Look, here is the Christ!' or 'Look, there he is!' do not *believe* it.
14. Whoever *believes* and is baptized will be saved, but whoever does not *believe* will be condemned.
15. And these signs will accompany those who *believe*:
16. The ones along the path are those who have heard; then the devil comes and takes away the word from their hearts, so that they may not *believe* and be saved.
17. But these have no root; they *believe* for a while, and in time of testing fall away.
18. Do not fear; only *believe*, and she will be well.
19. If I tell you, you will not *believe*, and if I ask you, you will not answer.

God said you cannot:
perish or be lost • John 10:28

20. O foolish ones, and slow of heart to *believe* all that the prophets have spoken!
21. And while they still *disbelieved* for joy and were marveling,
22. Because I said to you, 'I saw you under the fig tree,' do you *believe*? You will see greater things than these.
23. If I have told you earthly things and you do not *believe*, how can you *believe* if I tell you heavenly things?
24. that whoever *believes* in him may have eternal life.
25. that whoever *believes* in him should not perish but have eternal life.
26. Whoever *believes* in him is not condemned, but whoever does not *believe* is condemned already, because he has not *believed* in the name of the only Son of God.
27. Woman, *believe* me, the hour is coming when neither on this mountain nor in Jerusalem will you worship the Father.
28. Unless you see signs and wonders you will not *believe*.
29. "Go; your son will live." The man *believed* the word that Jesus spoke to him and went on his way.
30. Your son will live." And he himself *believed*, and all his household.

God said you cannot:
be moved • Psalm 16:8

31. Truly, truly, I say to you, whoever hears my word and **believes** him who sent me has eternal life.
32. and you do not have his word abiding in you, for you do not **believe** the one whom he has sent.
33. How can you **believe**, when you receive glory from one another and do not seek the glory that comes from the only God?
34. For if you **believed** Moses, you would **believe** me; for he wrote of me.
35. But if you do not **believe** his writings, how will you **believe** my words?
36. This is the work of God, that you **believe** in him whom he has sent.
37. I am the bread of life; whoever comes to me shall not hunger, and whoever **believes** in me shall never thirst.
38. But I said to you that you have seen me and yet do not **believe**.
39. For this is the will of my Father, that everyone who looks on the Son and **believes** in him should have eternal life, and I will raise him up on the last day.
40. Truly, truly, I say to you, whoever **believes** has eternal life.
41. But there are some of you who do not **believe**.
42. Whoever **believes** in me, as the Scripture has said,

God said **you cannot**:
be taken out of my Father's hand • John 10:29

'Out of his heart will flow rivers of living water.'
43. I told you that you would die in your sins, for unless you **believe** that I am he you will die in your sins.
44. So Jesus said to the Jews who had **believed** him, "If you abide in my word, you are truly my disciples, and you will know the truth, and the truth will set you free."
45. But because I tell the truth, you do not **believe** me.
46. Which one of you convicts me of sin? If I tell the truth, why do you not **believe** me?
47. Do you **believe** in the Son of Man?
48. I told you, and you do not **believe**. The works that I do in my Father's name bear witness about me, but you do not **believe** because you are not among my sheep.
49. If I am not doing the works of my Father, then do not **believe** me;
50. but if I do them, even though you do not **believe** me, **believe** the works,
51. and for your sake I am glad that I was not there, so that you may **believe**.

I am the resurrection and the life. Whoever **believes** in me, though he die, yet shall he live, and everyone who lives and **believes** in me shall never die. Do you **believe** this?

God said you cannot:
be charged or accused • Romans 8:33

52. Did I not tell you that if you *believed* you would see the glory of God?
53. I knew that you always hear me, but I said this on account of the people standing around, that they may *believe* that you sent me.
54. While you have the light, *believe* in the light, that you may become sons of light.
55. Whoever *believes* in me, *believes* not in me but in him who sent me.
56. I have come into the world as light, so that whoever *believes* in me may not remain in darkness.
57. I am telling you this now, before it takes place, that when it does take place you may *believe* that I am he.
58. Let not your hearts be troubled. *Believe* in God; *believe* also in me.
59. Do you not *believe* that I am in the Father and the Father is in me?
60. *Believe* me that I am in the Father and the Father is in me, or else *believe* on account of the works themselves.
61. Truly, truly, I say to you, whoever *believes* in me will also do the works that I do; and greater works than these will he do, because I am going to the Father.

God said you cannot:
be condemned along with the world • 1 Cor 11:32

62. And now I have told you before it takes place, so that when it does take place you may *believe*.
63. And when he comes, he will convict the world concerning sin and righteousness and judgment: concerning sin, because they do not *believe* in me;
64. for the Father himself loves you, because you have loved me and have *believed* that I came from God.
65. Do you now *believe*?
66. For I have given them the words that you gave me, and they have received them and have come to know in truth that I came from you; and they have *believed* that you sent me.
67. I do not ask for these only, but also for those who will *believe* in me through their word, that they may all be one, just as you, Father, are in me, and I in you, that they also may be in us, so that the world may *believe* that you have sent me.
68. Put your finger here, and see my hands; and put out your hand, and place it in my side. Do not *disbelieve*, but *believe*.
69. Have you *believed* because you have seen me?
70. Blessed are those who have not seen and yet have *believed*.

choose to believe!
choose believe

God said you are:
sanctified • 1 Cor 6:11

BElieVE

Don't listen to the lie. choose believe.

Jesus said, "My sheep hear my voice and a stranger's they won't follow."

This means Christians hear voices every day. There are times when the stranger's voice come from the words in a book.

There are times when the stranger's voice sound like the words you hear in a "good" video. Luckily, you get to choose which words to believe. Let the Bible be your filter for what you hear.

On the following pages, look for and believe all of the words that refer to
Who you ARE NOW vs
Who you WERE!

God said you are:
loved eternally • 1 Peter 1:5

peter

Towards the back of God's love letter to you, there's this guy named Peter who wrote some amazing words which are about you! I can't remember his words verbatim, but here are some key points Peter made concerning God's children.

Peter said,
- You **are** chosen
- You **have** grace and peace [that special sense of spiritual well-being] **are yours** in increasing abundance [as you walk closely with God]
- God's abundant and boundless mercy **has caused** us to be born again [that is, to be reborn from above—spiritually transformed, renewed, and set apart for His purpose] to an ever-living hope and confident assurance through the resurrection of Jesus Christ from the dead, [born anew] into an inheritance which is imperishable [beyond the reach of change] and undefiled and unfading, **reserved in heaven for you.**
- You **are being protected and shielded** by the power of God through your faith for salvation that is ready to be revealed [for you] in the last time.

God said you are:
kept by the power of God • 1 Peter 1:5

- Though you have not seen Him, you love Him; and though you do not even see Him now, **you believe** and trust in Him and you greatly rejoice and delight with inexpressible and glorious joy, **receiving as the result** [the outcome, the consummation] of your faith, the salvation of your soul.
- It was revealed to them that their services [their prophecies regarding grace] were not [meant] for themselves and their time, **but for you**, in these things [the death, resurrection, and glorification of Jesus Christ] which **have now been told to you** by those who **preached** the gospel to you by the [power of the] Holy Spirit [who was] sent from heaven.
- So prepare your minds for action, be completely **sober** [in spirit—steadfast, **self-disciplined**, spiritually and morally alert], fix your hope **completely** on the grace [of God] that is coming to you when Jesus Christ is revealed.
- [Live] as obedient children [of God]; do not be conformed to the evil desires **which governed** you in your ignorance [**before you knew** the requirements and transforming power of the good news regarding salvation].
- But like the Holy One **who called you**, be holy yourselves in all your conduct [be set apart

God said you are:
not condemned • Romans 8:1-2

from the world by your godly character and moral courage];
- "You shall be holy (set apart), for I am holy."
- For you know that you *were not redeemed* from your useless [spiritually unproductive] way of life inherited [by tradition] from your forefathers with perishable things like silver and gold,
- but [*you were actually purchased*] with precious blood, like that of a [sacrificial] lamb unblemished and spotless, the priceless blood of Christ.
- through Him *you believe* [confidently] in God [the heavenly Father], who raised Him from the dead and gave Him glory, so that your faith and hope are [*centered and rest*] in God.
- Since by your obedience to the truth *you have* purified *yourselves* for a sincere love of the believers, [see that you] love one another from the heart [always unselfishly seeking the best for one another],
- for *you have been born again* [that is, reborn from above—spiritually *transformed*, *renewed*, and *set apart* for His purpose]

(1 Peter 1)

God said you are:
one with the Lord • 1 Cor 6:17

paul

Towards the back of God's love letter to you, there's this guy named Paul who wrote some amazing words which are about you! I can't remember his words verbatim, but here are some key points Paul made concerning God's children.

Paul said,
- You **are a saint** (God's people)
- You **have grace and peace** [inner calm and spiritual well-being] from God your Father and the Lord Jesus Christ
- God **has blessed** you with **every** spiritual blessing in the heavenly realms in Christ
- [in His love] He **chose** you in Christ [actually **selected** you for Himself as His own] **before** the foundation of the world, so that we would be holy [that is, consecrated, set apart for Him, purpose-driven] and blameless in His sight.
- In love He **predestined** and lovingly **planned** for you to be **adopted** to Himself as [His own] children through Jesus Christ
-

God said you are:
on your way to heaven • John 14:6

- His glorious grace and favor, which He so freely bestowed on you in the Beloved [His Son, Jesus Christ]
- In Him you have redemption [that is, our deliverance and salvation] through His blood, [which paid the penalty for our sin and resulted in] the forgiveness and complete pardon of your sin, in accordance with the riches of His grace which He lavished on you.
- In Him also we have received an inheritance [a destiny—we were claimed by God as His own], having been predestined (chosen, appointed beforehand) according to the purpose of Him who works everything in agreement with the counsel and design of His will
- So that you who were the first to hope in Christ [who first put our confidence in Him as our Lord and Savior] would exist to the praise of His glory
- In Him, you also, when you heard the word of truth, the good news of your salvation, and [as a result] believed in Him, were stamped with the seal of the promised Holy Spirit [the One promised by Christ] as owned and protected [by God]
-

God said you are:
quickened by his mighty power • Eph 2:1

- The Spirit is the guarantee [the first installment, the pledge, a foretaste] of our inheritance until the redemption of God's own [**purchased**] possession [His believers]
- The eyes of your heart [the very center and core of your being] may be enlightened [flooded with light by the Holy Spirit], so that you will know and cherish the hope [the divine guarantee, the confident expectation] to which He has called you, the riches of His glorious inheritance in the **saints** (God's people), and [so that you will begin to know] what the immeasurable and unlimited and surpassing greatness of His [**active**, spiritual] power is in us who **believe**
- These are in accordance with the working of His mighty strength which He **produced** in Christ **when He raised** Him from the dead and **seated** Him at His own right hand in the heavenly places
- He **put** all things [in every realm] in subjection under Christ's feet, and **appointed** Him as [supreme and authoritative] head over all things in the church, which is His body, the fullness of Him who fills and **completes all things** in all [**believers**].

(Ephesians 1)

God said you are:
seated in heavenly places • Eph 1:3

paul

In the second half of God's love letter to you, Paul wrote some freeing words which are about you! I can't remember these words verbatim either, but here are some key points Paul made concerning God's children.

Paul said,

- When you *were children* (spiritually immature), *were* kept like slaves under the elementary [man-made religious or philosophical] teachings of the world.
- But when [in God's plan] the proper time had fully come, God sent His Son, born of a woman, born under the [regulations of the] Law, so that He might redeem and liberate those who *were under the Law*, that we [who *believe*] might be adopted as sons [as God's children with all rights as fully grown members of a family].
- And because you [really] are [His] sons, God *has sent the Spirit of His Son into our hearts*, crying out, "Abba! Father!"

God said you are:
hidden with Christ in God • Psalm 32:7

- Therefore **you are no longer a slave** (bond-servant), but a son; and if a son, then also an heir through [the gracious act of] God [through Christ].
- But at that time, **when you did not know** [the true] God and **were unacquainted** with Him, you [Gentiles] **were slaves** to those [pagan] things which by [their very] nature were not and could not be gods at all.
- Now, however, since **you have come to know** [the true] God [through personal experience], or rather to be known by God, how is it that you are turning back again to the weak and worthless elemental principles [of religions and philosophies], to which you want to be enslaved all over again?
- **Believers**, I beg of you, become as I am [free from the bondage of Jewish ritualism and ordinances], for I have become as you are [a Gentile].
- And you, [**believing**] brothers and sisters, like Isaac, **are children** [not merely of physical descent, like Ishmael, but are children born]
- So then, **believers**, we [who **are born again**—reborn from above—**spiritually transformed, renewed**, and **set apart** for His purpose]

God said you are:
protected from the evil one • 1 John 5:18

- It was for this *freedom that Christ set you free* [completely liberating you]; therefore keep standing firm and do not be subject again to a yoke of slavery [*which you once removed*].
- You have been severed from Christ, *if you seek to be* [a]justified [that is, declared free of the guilt of sin and its penalty, and placed in right standing with God] through the Law; you have fallen from grace [for you have lost your grasp on God's unmerited favor and blessing].
- For you [not relying on the Law but] through the [strength and power of the Holy] Spirit, by faith, are waiting [confidently] for the hope of righteousness [the completion of our salvation].
- For [if you are] in Christ Jesus neither circumcision nor uncircumcision means anything, but only faith activated and expressed and working through love.
- You were running [the race] well; who has interfered and prevented you from obeying the truth? This [deceptive] persuasion is not from Him who *called you* [to freedom in Christ].
- A little leaven [a slight inclination to error, or a few false teachers] leavens the whole batch [it perverts the concept of faith and misleads the church].

God said you are:
kept by the power of God • 1 Peter 1:5

- I have confidence in you in the Lord that you will adopt no other view [contrary to mine on the matter]; but the one who is disturbing you, whoever he is, will have to bear the penalty.
- But as for me, **believers**, if I am still preaching circumcision [as I had done before I met Christ; and as some accuse me of doing now, as necessary for salvation],
- For you, my **believers, were called to freedom**; only do not let your freedom become an opportunity for the sinful nature (worldliness, selfishness), but through love serve and seek the best for one another.
- But I say, walk habitually in the [Holy] Spirit [seek Him and be responsive to His guidance], and then you **will certainly not carry out the desire of the sinful nature** [which responds impulsively without regard for God and His precepts].
- For the sinful nature has its desire which is opposed to the Spirit, and the [desire of the] Spirit opposes the [h]sinful nature; for these [two, the sinful nature and the Spirit] are in direct opposition to each other [continually in conflict], so that you [**as believers**] do not [always] do whatever [good things] you want to do.

God said you are:
secure in Christ • Jn 10:28-29

- But if you are *guided and led* by the Spirit, *you are not subject to the Law.*
- Now *the practices of the sinful nature* are clearly evident: they are sexual immorality, impurity, sensuality (total irresponsibility, lack of self-control), idolatry, sorcery, hostility, strife, jealousy, fits of anger, disputes, dissensions, factions [that promote heresies], envy, drunkenness, riotous behavior, and other things like these.
- I warn you beforehand, just as I did previously, that those *who practice such things* will not inherit the kingdom of God.
- But the fruit of the Spirit [*the result of His presence within us*] is love [unselfish concern for others], joy, [inner] peace, patience [not the ability to wait, but how we act while waiting], kindness, goodness, faithfulness, gentleness, self-control. Against such things there is no law.
- And those *who belong* to Christ Jesus *have* crucified the sinful nature together with its passions and appetites.
- If we [claim to] live by the [Holy] Spirit, we must also walk by the Spirit [with personal integrity, godly character, and moral courage—our conduct *empowered by the Holy Spirit*].

(Galatians 4 & 5)

God said you are:
set on a Rock • Psalm 40:2

john

At the back of God's love letter to you, there's this guy named John who wrote some encouraging words which are about you! I can't remember his words verbatim, but here are some key points John made concerning God's children.

John said,
- My little child (**believer**, dear one),
- I am writing you these things so that you **will not sin** and violate God's law.
- And **if** you sin, **you have an Advocate** [who will intercede for us] with the Father: Jesus Christ the righteous [the upright, the just One, who conforms to the Father's will in every way—purpose, thought, and action].
- And He [that same Jesus] is the propitiation for your sins [the atoning sacrifice that holds back the wrath of God that would otherwise be directed at us because of your sinful nature—your worldliness, our lifestyle]; and not for yours alone, but also for [the sins of all **believers** throughout] the whole world.

God said you are:
the head and not the tail • Deut 28:13

- And this is how you know [daily, by experience] that you have come to know Him [to understand Him and be more deeply acquainted with Him]:
- if you habitually keep [focused on His precepts and obey] His commandments (teachings).
- Whoever says, "I have come to know Him," but does not habitually keep [focused on His precepts and obey] His commandments (teachings), is a liar, and the truth [of the divine word] is not in him. But whoever habitually keeps His word and obeys His precepts [and treasures His message in its entirety], in him the love of God has truly been perfected [it is completed and has reached maturity]. By this we know [for certain] that we are in Him:
- Whoever says he lives in Christ [that is, whoever says he has accepted Him as God and Savior] ought [as a moral obligation] to walk and conduct himself just as He walked and conducted Himself.
- Beloved, I am not writing a new commandment to you, but an old commandment which you have had from the beginning; the old commandment is the message which you have heard [before from us].
- On the other hand, I am writing a new com-

God said you are:
light in the darkness • Matthew 5:14

mandment to you, which is true and **realized** in Christ and in you, because the darkness [of moral blindness] is clearing away and the true Light [the revelation of God in Christ] is **already** shining.

- The one who says he is in the Light [in consistent fellowship with Christ] and yet [a]habitually hates (works against) his brother [in Christ] is in the darkness until now.
- The one who loves and unselfishly seeks the best for his [**believing**] brother lives in the Light, and in him there is **no occasion for stumbling or offense** [he does not hurt the cause of Christ or lead others to sin].
- But the one who habitually hates (works against) his brother [in Christ] is in [spiritual] darkness and is walking in the darkness, and does not know where he is going because the darkness has blinded his eyes.
- I am writing to you, little children (**believers**, dear ones), because your sins **have been forgiven** for His name's sake [**you have been pardoned** and **released** from spiritual debt through His name because you **have confessed** His name, believing in Him as Savior].

God said you are:
a city set on a hill • Matthew 5:14

- I am writing to you, fathers [those **believers** who are spiritually mature], because you **know Him** who has existed from the beginning.
- I am writing to you, young men [those **believers** who are growing in spiritual maturity], because you **have been victorious** and **have overcome the evil one**.
- I have written to you, children [those who are new **believers**, those spiritually immature], because you **have come to know the Father**.
- I have written to you, fathers, because **you know Him** who has existed from the beginning.
- I have written to you, young men, because you **are strong and vigorous**, and the word of God **remains [always]** in you, and **you have been victorious** over the evil one [by accepting Jesus as Savior].
- All that is in the world—the lust and sensual craving of the flesh and the lust and longing of the eyes and the boastful pride of life [pretentious confidence in one's resources or in the stability of earthly things]—these do not come from the Father, but are from the world.

God said you are:
salt of the earth • Matthew 5:13

- The world is passing away, and with it its lusts [the shameful pursuits and ungodly longings]; but the one who does the will of God and carries out His purposes lives forever.
- But you **have an anointing** from the Holy One [**you have been set apart**, specially **gifted and prepared** by the Holy Spirit], and all of you know [the truth because He teaches us, illuminates our minds, and guards us from error].
- I **have not written to you because you do not know the truth**, but because **you do know it**, and because no lie [nothing false, no deception] is of the truth.
- As for you, let that **remain in you** [keeping in your hearts that message of salvation] which **you heard** from the beginning. If what you **heard from the beginning** remains in you, **you too will remain** in the Son and in the Father [forever].
- This is the promise which He Himself **promised us**—eternal life.
- These things I **have written to you** with reference to those who are trying to deceive you [seducing you and leading you away from the truth and sound doctrine].

God said you are:
his sheep • Psalm 23

- As for you, the anointing [the special gift, the preparation] *which you received* from Him *remains [permanently]* in you, and *you have no need for anyone to teach you*. But just as His anointing teaches you [*giving you insight* through the presence of the Holy Spirit] *about all things*, and is true and is not a lie, and just as His anointing *has taught you*, *you must remain* in Him [being rooted in Him, knit to Him].
- Now, little children (*believers*, dear ones), *remain* in Him [with unwavering faith], so that when He appears [at His return], we may have [perfect] confidence and not be ashamed and shrink away from Him at His coming.
- If you know that He is absolutely righteous, you know [for certain] that everyone who practices righteousness [doing what is right and conforming to God's will] *has been born* of Him.

(1 John 2)

God said you are:
a citizen of heaven • 1 Peter 2:11

jude

At the very back of God's love letter to you, Jude wrote some liberating words which are about you! I can't remember his words verbatim either, but here are some key points Jude made concerning God's children.

Jude said,
- To those who **are the called** (God's chosen ones, the elect), **dearly loved** by God the Father, and **kept** [secure and set apart] for Jesus Christ:
- May mercy and peace and love be multiplied to you [filling your heart with the spiritual well-being and serenity experienced by those who walk closely with God].

Beloved, while I was making every effort to write you about **our common salvation**, I was compelled to write to you [urgently] appealing that you fight strenuously for [the defense of] the faith **which was once for all handed down** to the **saints** [the faith that is the sum

---

God said you are:
more-than-a-conqueror • Romans 8:37

of Christian **belief** that **was given** verbally to **believers**].

- Now I want to remind you, although **you are fully informed once for all**, that the Lord, after saving a people out of the land of Egypt, subsequently destroyed those who did not **believe** [who refused to trust and obey and rely on Him].

- But as for you, **beloved**, remember the [prophetic] words spoken by the apostles of our Lord Jesus Christ.

- But you, **beloved**, build yourselves up on [the foundation of] your most holy faith [continually progress, rise like an edifice higher and higher], pray in the Holy Spirit, and **keep yourselves** in the love of God, waiting anxiously and looking forward to the mercy of our Lord Jesus Christ [which will bring you] to eternal life.

- Now to Him **who is able to keep you** from stumbling or falling into sin, and to present you **unblemished** [**blameless** and **faultless**] in the presence of His glory with triumphant joy and unspeakable delight, to the only God our Savior, through Jesus Christ our Lord, be glory, majesty, dominion, and power, before all time and now and forever. Amen.

God said you are:
born again • 1 Peter 1:23

survey

I created an online survey a while back and asked people who are in "recovery" to answers a few questions.

Although there are things in some of their answers that are worth "celebrating," you might notice one thing that runs consistently through everyone's answers.

God said you are:
a victor • 1 John 5:4

ronny

5 Questions:

How man clean days you have?
90+2117+545+555

How long have you been in "recovery"?
20 years

How much longer will you be going?
rest of my life

Would you consider not going to any meetings for six months?
no answer

What's something you've always wanted to do?
Parachute or wing suit.

What do you look forward to?
Snowboarding, concerts, church, time with my family, laughing

God said you are:
healed by his stripes • Is 53:6

heather

5 Questions:

How man clean days you have?
5493

How long have you been in "recovery"?
15 years

How much longer will you be going?
unknown

Would you consider not going to any meetings for six months?
no answer

What's something you've always wanted to do?
Go on a cruise.

What do you look forward to?
Each new day

God said you are:
covered by blood of Jesus • Rev 12:11

che

5 Questions:

How man clean days you have?
53 years

How long have you been in "recovery"?
Learned grace - since teens

How much longer will you be going?
for the rest of my life

Would you consider not going to any meetings for six months?
no answer

What's something you've always wanted to do?
1. Be an astronaut. 2. Solve nuclear fusion

What do you look forward to?
Sharing God's grace

God said you are:
sheltered under his wing • Psalm 91:4

autum

5 Questions:

How man clean days you have?
496 days

How long have you been in "recovery"?
16 months

How much longer will you be going?
for the rest of my life

Would you consider not going to any meetings for six months?
no answer

What's something you've always wanted to do?
Start a family. Travel and get married

What do you look forward to?
Waking up clean. Life in general

God said you are:
free forever from sin's power • Romans 6:14

brittney

5 Questions:

How man clean days you have?
1101 days

How long have you been in "recovery"?
3 years

How much longer will you be going?
forever

Would you consider not going to any meetings for six months?
no answer

What's something you've always wanted to do?
Go skydiving

What do you look forward to?
Waking up each day clean and sober and reaching my goals.

God said you are:
united with the Lord • 1 Corinthians 6:17

danny

5 Questions:

How man clean days you have?
4015 days

How long have you been in "recovery"?
4 years

How much longer will you be going?
on GoinG

Would you consider not going to any meetings for six months?
no answer

What's something you've always wanted to do?
Become a web developer but before that, being used by Christ.

What do you look forward to?
Growing closer in Christ.

God said you are:
a member of Christ's Body • 1 Corinthians 12:27

the barn

Years ago a man was going away on business for a week. He told his worker, "While I'm gone, I'd like for you to paint the barn."

The following week when the man returned, he asked his worker, "While I was gone, did you paint the barn?"

His worker replied, "I wrote down what you said. Then I read it every morning before work."

The man replied, "Ok. But, did you paint the barn?"

His worker said, "Well, one day I had a few friends over, and we had a meeting in the barn. We talked about all the ways we could paint the barn."

The man said, "So, after your meeting, did you paint the barn?"

The worker replied, "My friends and I agreed that it would be best if we went home and looked over our barn-painting notes from the meeting until next week's meeting."

God said you are:
established • 2 Corinthians 1:21

The following week, each of the worker's friends brought a friend with them to the barn to hear what the worker had to say about the painting the barn. The turnout was so glorious that the worker decided to create a seven-week series called,
7 Habits of Highly Effective Barn Painters.

Week after week, more and more people showed up. The worker was so excited.

Two months later the worker told the man, "You're not going to believe this; there were 120 people in the barn tonight! They all came to hear my talk on barn painting!"

The man smiled and said,
"So, did you guys paint the barn?"

The worker said, "Even better! Because we no longer have enough room for everyone in the barn, we decided to open another barn down the road."

The man replied, "Before you open another barn, shouldn't you first paint the barn?"

The worker said,

"Oh! We're way too busy now to paint the barn!"

God said you are:
a branch of the true vine • John 15:1,5

be and do

Your BE (WHO) produces your DO.
It can't help but to.

Most of the time, those who don't know what to do, or "who they want to be when they grow up" are the same ones who lack true identity. However, if no one has told them, how would they know?

I met a stranger at Starbucks who told me, "I believe the reason why the church today doesn't look like the church in the Bible is because His followers today don't know what He said."

Ouch. Could he have been right? Unfortunately, I think he was. This concerned me because when he made that statement, I couldn't think of eight things Jesus said for us to do. I then began a long but eye-opening journey as I took the time to highlight some of the things Jesus said.

Read, skim, or flip through the pages of this book, and look for these highlighted sections. As you do this and read the words of Jesus for yourself, you might see things you've never seen before.

> The Scriptures say, "I believed, so I spoke." Our faith is like that too. We believe, and so we speak. • 2 Corinthians 4:13

matthew

Matthew 3:15
But Jesus answered him, "Let it be so now, for thus it is fitting for us to fulfill all righteousness." Then he consented.

Matthew 4:4
But he answered, "It is written, " 'Man shall not live by bread alone, but by every word that comes from the mouth of God.' "

Matthew 4:7
Jesus said to him, "Again it is written, 'You shall not put the Lord your God to the test.' "

Matthew 4:10
Then Jesus said to him, "Be gone, Satan! For it is written, " 'You shall worship the Lord your God and him only shall you serve.' "

Matthew 4:17
From that time Jesus began to preach, saying, "Repent, for the kingdom of heaven is at hand."

Matthew 4:19
And he said to them, "Follow me, and I will make you fishers of men."

Matthew 5:3
"Blessed are the poor in spirit, for theirs is the kingdom of heaven.

He Does • You Do • You Don't • Kingdom

Matthew 5:4
"Blessed are those who mourn, for they shall be comforted.

Matthew 5:5
"Blessed are the meek, for they shall inherit the earth.

Matthew 5:6
"Blessed are those who hunger and thirst for righteousness, for they shall be satisfied.

Matthew 5:7
"Blessed are the merciful, for they shall receive mercy.

Matthew 5:8
"Blessed are the pure in heart, for they shall see God.

Matthew 5:9
"Blessed are the peacemakers, for they shall be called sons of God.

Matthew 5:10
"Blessed are those who are persecuted for righteousness' sake, for theirs is the kingdom of heaven.

Matthew 5:11
"Blessed are you when others revile you and persecute you and utter all kinds of evil against you falsely on my account.

Matthew 5:12
Rejoice and be glad, for your reward is great in heaven, for so they persecuted the prophets who were before you.

Matthew 5:13
"You are the salt of the earth, but if salt has lost its taste, how shall its saltiness be restored? It is no longer good for anything except to be thrown out and trampled under people's feet.

Matthew 5:14
"You are the light of the world. A city set on a hill cannot be hidden.

Matthew 5:15
Nor do people light a lamp and put it under a basket, but on a stand, and it gives light to all in the house.

Matthew 5:16
In the same way, let your light shine before others, so that they may see your good works and give glory to your Father who is in heaven.

Matthew 5:17
"Do not think that I have come to abolish the Law or the Prophets; I have not come to abolish them but to fulfill them.

Matthew 5:18
For truly, I say to you, until heaven and earth pass away, not an iota, not a dot, will pass from the Law until all is accomplished.

Matthew 5:19
Therefore whoever relaxes one of the least of these commandments and teaches others to do the same will be called least in the kingdom of heaven, but whoever does them and teaches them will be called great in the kingdom of heaven.

Matthew 5:20
For I tell you, unless your righteousness exceeds that of the scribes and Pharisees, you will never enter the kingdom of heaven.

Matthew 5:21
"You have heard that it was said to those of old, 'You shall not murder; and whoever murders will be liable to judgment.'

Matthew 5:22
But I say to you that everyone who is angry with his brother will be liable to judgment; whoever insults his brother will be liable to the council; and whoever says, 'You fool!' will be liable to the hell of fire.

Matthew 5:23
So if you are offering your gift at the altar and there remember that your brother has something against you,

Matthew 5:24
leave your gift there before the altar and go. First be reconciled to your brother, and then come and offer your gift.

Matthew 5:25
Come to terms quickly with your accuser while you are going with him to court, lest your accuser hand you over to the judge, and the judge to the guard, and you be put in prison.

Matthew 5:26
Truly, I say to you, you will never get out until you have paid the last penny.

Matthew 5:27
"You have heard that it was said, 'You shall not commit adultery.'

Matthew 5:28
But I say to you that everyone who looks at a woman with lustful intent has already committed adultery with her in his heart.

Matthew 5:29
If your right eye causes you to sin, tear it out and throw it away. For it is better that you lose one of your members than that your whole body be thrown into hell.

Matthew 5:30
And if your right hand causes you to sin, cut it off and throw it away. For it is better that you lose one of your members than that your whole body go into hell.

Matthew 5:31
"It was also said, 'Whoever divorces his wife, let him give her a certificate of divorce.'

Matthew 5:32
But I say to you that everyone who divorces his wife, except on the ground of sexual immorality, makes her commit adultery, and whoever marries a divorced woman commits adultery.

Matthew 5:33
"Again you have heard that it was said to those of old, 'You shall not swear falsely, but shall perform to the Lord what you have sworn.'

Matthew 5:34
But I say to you, Do not take an oath at all, either by

heaven, for it is the throne of God,

Matthew 5:35
or by the earth, for it is his footstool, or by Jerusalem, for it is the city of the great King.

Matthew 5:36
And do not take an oath by your head, for you cannot make one hair white or black.

Matthew 5:37
Let what you say be simply 'Yes' or 'No'; anything more than this comes from evil.

Matthew 5:38
"You have heard that it was said, 'An eye for an eye and a tooth for a tooth.'

Matthew 5:39
But I say to you, Do not resist the one who is evil. But if anyone slaps you on the right cheek, turn to him the other also.

Matthew 5:40
And if anyone would sue you and take your tunic, let him have your cloak as well.

Matthew 5:41
And if anyone forces you to go one mile, go with him two miles.

Matthew 5:42
Give to the one who begs from you, and do not refuse the one who would borrow from you.

Matthew 5:43
"You have heard that it was said, 'You shall love your neighbor and hate your enemy.'

Matthew 5:44
But I say to you, Love your enemies and pray for those who persecute you,

Matthew 5:45
so that you may be sons of your Father who is in heaven. For he makes his sun rise on the evil and on the good, and sends rain on the just and on the unjust.

Matthew 5:46
For if you love those who love you, what reward do you have? Do not even the tax collectors do the same?

Matthew 5:47
And if you greet only your brothers, what more are you doing than others? Do not even the Gentiles do the same?

Matthew 5:48
You therefore must be perfect, as your heavenly Father is perfect.

Matthew 6:1
"Beware of practicing your righteousness before other people in order to be seen by them, for then you will have no reward from your Father who is in heaven.

Matthew 6:2
"Thus, when you give to the needy, sound no trumpet before you, as the hypocrites do in the synagogues and in the streets, that they may be praised by others. Truly,

I say to you, they have received their reward.

Matthew 6:3
But when you give to the needy, do not let your left hand know what your right hand is doing,

Matthew 6:4
so that your giving may be in secret. And your Father who sees in secret will reward you.

Matthew 6:5
"And when you pray, you must not be like the hypocrites. For they love to stand and pray in the synagogues and at the street corners, that they may be seen by others. Truly, I say to you, they have received their reward.

Matthew 6:6
But when you pray, go into your room and shut the door and pray to your Father who is in secret. And your Father who sees in secret will reward you.

Matthew 6:7
"And when you pray, do not heap up empty phrases as the Gentiles do, for they think that they will be heard for their many words.

Matthew 6:8
Do not be like them, for your Father knows what you need before you ask him.

Matthew 6:9
Pray then like this: "Our Father in heaven, hallowed be your name.

Matthew 6:10
Your kingdom come, your will be done, on earth as it is in heaven.

Matthew 6:11
Give us this day our daily bread,

Matthew 6:12
and forgive us our debts, as we also have forgiven our debtors.

Matthew 6:13
And lead us not into temptation, but deliver us from evil.

Matthew 6:14
For if you forgive others their trespasses, your heavenly Father will also forgive you,

Matthew 6:15
but if you do not forgive others their trespasses, neither will your Father forgive your trespasses.

Matthew 6:16
"And when you fast, do not look gloomy like the hypocrites, for they disfigure their faces that their fasting may be seen by others. Truly, I say to you, they have received their reward.

Matthew 6:17
But when you fast, anoint your head and wash your face,

Matthew 6:18
that your fasting may not be seen by others but by your Father who is in secret. And your Father who sees in

secret will reward you.

Matthew 6:19
"Do not lay up for yourselves treasures on earth, where moth and rust destroy and where thieves break in and steal,

Matthew 6:20
but lay up for yourselves treasures in heaven, where neither moth nor rust destroys and where thieves do not break in and steal.

Matthew 6:21
For where your treasure is, there your heart will be also.

Matthew 6:22
"The eye is the lamp of the body. So, if your eye is healthy, your whole body will be full of light,

Matthew 6:23
but if your eye is bad, your whole body will be full of darkness. If then the light in you is darkness, how great is the darkness!

Matthew 6:24
"No one can serve two masters, for either he will hate the one and love the other, or he will be devoted to the one and despise the other. You cannot serve God and money.

Matthew 6:25
"Therefore I tell you, do not be anxious about your life, what you will eat or what you will drink, nor about your body, what you will put on. Is not life more than food, and the body more than clothing?

Matthew 6:26
Look at the birds of the air: they neither sow nor reap nor gather into barns, and yet your heavenly Father feeds them. Are you not of more value than they?

Matthew 6:27
And which of you by being anxious can add a single hour to his span of life?

Matthew 6:28
And why are you anxious about clothing? Consider the lilies of the field, how they grow: they neither toil nor spin,

Matthew 6:29
yet I tell you, even Solomon in all his glory was not arrayed like one of these.

Matthew 6:30
But if God so clothes the grass of the field, which today is alive and tomorrow is thrown into the oven, ==will he not much more clothe you==, O you of little faith?

Matthew 6:31
Therefore do not be anxious, saying, 'What shall we eat?' or 'What shall we drink?' or 'What shall we wear?'

Matthew 6:32
For the Gentiles seek after all these things, and your heavenly Father knows that you need them all.

Matthew 6:33
But ==seek first== the kingdom of God and ==his righteousness==, and all these things ==will be added to you==.

Matthew 6:34
"Therefore do not be anxious about tomorrow, for tomorrow will be anxious for itself. Sufficient for the day is its own trouble.

Matthew 7:1
"Judge not, that you be not judged.

Matthew 7:2
For with the judgment you pronounce you will be judged, and with the measure you use it will be measured to you.

Matthew 7:3
Why do you see the speck that is in your brother's eye, but do not notice the log that is in your own eye?

Matthew 7:4
Or how can you say to your brother, 'Let me take the speck out of your eye,' when there is the log in your own eye?

Matthew 7:5
You hypocrite, first take the log out of your own eye, and then you will see clearly to take the speck out of your brother's eye.

Matthew 7:6
"Do not give dogs what is holy, and do not throw your pearls before pigs, lest they trample them underfoot and turn to attack you.

Matthew 7:7
"Ask, and it will be given to you; seek, and you will find; knock, and it will be opened to you.

Matthew 7:8
For everyone who asks receives, and the one who seeks finds, and to the one who knocks it will be opened.

Matthew 7:9
Or which one of you, if his son asks him for bread, will give him a stone?

Matthew 7:10
Or if he asks for a fish, will give him a serpent?

Matthew 7:11
If you then, who are evil, know how to give good gifts to your children, how much more will your Father who is in heaven give good things to those who ask him!

Matthew 7:12
"So whatever you wish that others would do to you, do also to them, for this is the Law and the Prophets.

Matthew 7:13
"Enter by the narrow gate. For the gate is wide and the way is easy that leads to destruction, and those who enter by it are many.

Matthew 7:14
For the gate is narrow and the way is hard that leads to life, and those who find it are few.

Matthew 7:15
"Beware of false prophets, who come to you in sheep's clothing but inwardly are ravenous wolves.

Matthew 7:16
You will recognize them by their fruits. Are grapes gath-

ered from thornbushes, or figs from thistles?

Matthew 7:17
So, every healthy tree bears good fruit, but the diseased tree bears bad fruit.

Matthew 7:18
A healthy tree cannot bear bad fruit, nor can a diseased tree bear good fruit.

Matthew 7:19
Every tree that does not bear good fruit is cut down and thrown into the fire.

Matthew 7:20
Thus you will recognize them by their fruits.

Matthew 7:21
"Not everyone who says to me, 'Lord, Lord,' will enter the kingdom of heaven, but the one who does the will of my Father who is in heaven.

Matthew 7:22
On that day many will say to me, 'Lord, Lord, did we not prophesy in your name, and cast out demons in your name, and do many mighty works in your name?'

Matthew 7:23
And then will I declare to them, 'I never knew you; depart from me, you workers of lawlessness.'

Matthew 7:24
"Everyone then who hears these words of mine and does them will be like a wise man who built his house on the rock.

Matthew 7:25
And the rain fell, and the floods came, and the winds blew and beat on that house, but it did not fall, because it had been founded on the rock.

Matthew 7:26
And everyone who hears these words of mine and does not do them will be like a foolish man who built his house on the sand.

Matthew 7:27
And the rain fell, and the floods came, and the winds blew and beat against that house, and it fell, and great was the fall of it."

Matthew 8:3
And Jesus stretched out his hand and touched him, saying, "I will; be clean." And immediately his leprosy was cleansed.

Matthew 8:4
And Jesus said to him, "See that you say nothing to anyone, but go, show yourself to the priest and offer the gift that Moses commanded, for a proof to them."

Matthew 8:7
And he said to him, "I will come and heal him."

Matthew 8:10
When Jesus heard this, he marveled and said to those who followed him, "Truly, I tell you, with no one in Israel have I found such faith.

Matthew 8:11
I tell you, many will come from east and west and

recline at table with Abraham, Isaac, and Jacob in the kingdom of heaven,

Matthew 8:12
while the sons of the kingdom will be thrown into the outer darkness. In that place there will be weeping and gnashing of teeth."

Matthew 8:13
And to the centurion Jesus said, "Go; let it be done for you as you have believed." And the servant was healed at that very moment.

Matthew 8:20
And Jesus said to him, "Foxes have holes, and birds of the air have nests, but the Son of Man has nowhere to lay his head."

Matthew 8:22
And Jesus said to him, "Follow me, and leave the dead to bury their own dead."

Matthew 8:26
And he said to them, "Why are you afraid, O you of little faith?" Then he rose and rebuked the winds and the sea, and there was a great calm.

Matthew 8:32
And he said to them, "Go." So they came out and went into the pigs, and behold, the whole herd rushed down the steep bank into the sea and drowned in the waters.

Matthew 9:2
And behold, some people brought to him a paralytic, lying on a bed. And when Jesus saw their faith, he said

to the paralytic, "Take heart, my son; your sins are forgiven."

Matthew 9:4
But Jesus, knowing their thoughts, said, "Why do you think evil in your hearts?

Matthew 9:5
For which is easier, to say, 'Your sins are forgiven,' or to say, 'Rise and walk'?

Matthew 9:6
But that you may know that the Son of Man has authority on earth to forgive sins"—he then said to the paralytic—"Rise, pick up your bed and go home."

Matthew 9:9
As Jesus passed on from there, he saw a man called Matthew sitting at the tax booth, and he said to him, "Follow me." And he rose and followed him.

Matthew 9:12
But when he heard it, he said, "Those who are well have no need of a physician, but those who are sick.

Matthew 9:13
Go and learn what this means, 'I desire mercy, and not sacrifice.' For I came not to call the righteous, but sinners."

Matthew 9:15
And Jesus said to them, "Can the wedding guests mourn as long as the bridegroom is with them? The days will come when the bridegroom is taken away from them, and then they will fast.

Matthew 9:16
No one puts a piece of unshrunk cloth on an old garment, for the patch tears away from the garment, and a worse tear is made.

Matthew 9:17
Neither is new wine put into old wineskins. If it is, the skins burst and the wine is spilled and the skins are destroyed. But new wine is put into fresh wineskins, and so both are preserved."

Matthew 9:22
Jesus turned, and seeing her he said, "Take heart, daughter; your faith has made you well." And instantly the woman was made well.

Matthew 9:24
he said, "Go away, for the girl is not dead but sleeping." And they laughed at him.

Matthew 9:28
When he entered the house, the blind men came to him, and Jesus said to them, "Do you believe that I am able to do this?" They said to him, "Yes, Lord."

Matthew 9:29
Then he touched their eyes, saying, "According to your faith be it done to you."

Matthew 9:30
And their eyes were opened. And Jesus sternly warned them, "See that no one knows about it."

Matthew 9:37
Then he said to his disciples, "The harvest is plentiful, but

the laborers are few;

Matthew 9:38
therefore pray earnestly to the Lord of the harvest to send out laborers into his harvest."

Matthew 10:5
These twelve Jesus sent out, instructing them, "Go nowhere among the Gentiles and enter no town of the Samaritans,

Matthew 10:6
but go rather to the lost sheep of the house of Israel.

Matthew 10:7
And proclaim as you go, saying, 'The kingdom of heaven is at hand.'

Matthew 10:8
Heal the sick, raise the dead, cleanse lepers, cast out demons. You received without paying; give without pay.

Matthew 10:9
Acquire no gold or silver or copper for your belts,

Matthew 10:10
no bag for your journey, or two tunics or sandals or a staff, for the laborer deserves his food.

Matthew 10:11
And whatever town or village you enter, find out who is worthy in it and stay there until you depart.

Matthew 10:12
As you enter the house, greet it.

Matthew 10:13
And if the house is worthy, let your peace come upon it, but if it is not worthy, let your peace return to you.

Matthew 10:14
And if anyone will not receive you or listen to your words, shake off the dust from your feet when you leave that house or town.

Matthew 10:15
Truly, I say to you, it will be more bearable on the day of judgment for the land of Sodom and Gomorrah than for that town.

Matthew 10:16
"Behold, I am sending you out as sheep in the midst of wolves, so be wise as serpents and innocent as doves.

Matthew 10:17
Beware of men, for they will deliver you over to courts and flog you in their synagogues,

Matthew 10:18
and you will be dragged before governors and kings for my sake, to bear witness before them and the Gentiles.

Matthew 10:19
When they deliver you over, do not be anxious how you are to speak or what you are to say, for what you are to say will be given to you in that hour.

Matthew 10:20
For it is not you who speak, but the Spirit of your Father speaking through you.

Matthew 10:21
Brother will deliver brother over to death, and the father his child, and children will rise against parents and have them put to death,

Matthew 10:22
and you will be hated by all for my name's sake. But the one who endures to the end will be saved.

Matthew 10:23
When they persecute you in one town, flee to the next, for truly, I say to you, you will not have gone through all the towns of Israel before the Son of Man comes.

Matthew 10:24
"A disciple is not above his teacher, nor a servant above his master.

Matthew 10:25
It is enough for the disciple to be like his teacher, and the servant like his master. If they have called the master of the house Beelzebul, how much more will they malign those of his household.

Matthew 10:26
"So have no fear of them, for nothing is covered that will not be revealed, or hidden that will not be known.

Matthew 10:27
What I tell you in the dark, say in the light, and what you hear whispered, proclaim on the housetops.

Matthew 10:28
And do not fear those who kill the body but cannot kill the soul. Rather fear him who can destroy both soul and

body in hell.

Matthew 10:29
Are not two sparrows sold for a penny? And not one of them will fall to the ground apart from your Father.

Matthew 10:30
But even the hairs of your head are all numbered.

Matthew 10:31
Fear not, therefore; you are of more value than many sparrows.

Matthew 10:32
So everyone who acknowledges me before men, I also will acknowledge before my Father who is in heaven,

Matthew 10:33
but whoever denies me before men, I also will deny before my Father who is in heaven.

Matthew 10:34
"Do not think that I have come to bring peace to the earth. I have not come to bring peace, but a sword.

Matthew 10:35
For I have come to set a man against his father, and a daughter against her mother, and a daughter-in-law against her mother-in-law.

Matthew 10:36
And a person's enemies will be those of his own household.

Matthew 10:37
Whoever loves father or mother more than me is not worthy of me, and whoever loves son or daughter more than me is not worthy of me.

Matthew 10:38
And whoever does not take his cross and follow me is not worthy of me.

Matthew 10:39
Whoever finds his life will lose it, and whoever loses his life for my sake will find it.

Matthew 10:40
"Whoever receives you receives me, and whoever receives me receives him who sent me.

Matthew 10:41
The one who receives a prophet because he is a prophet will receive a prophet's reward, and the one who receives a righteous person because he is a righteous person will receive a righteous person's reward.

Matthew 10:42
And whoever gives one of these little ones even a cup of cold water because he is a disciple, truly, I say to you, he will by no means lose his reward."

Matthew 11:4
And Jesus answered them, "Go and tell John what you hear and see:

Matthew 11:5
the blind receive their sight and the lame walk, lepers are cleansed and the deaf hear, and the dead are

==raised up==, and the poor have good news preached to them.

Matthew 11:6
And blessed is the one who is ~~not offended by me~~."

Matthew 11:7
As they went away, Jesus began to speak to the crowds concerning John: "What did you go out into the wilderness to see? A reed shaken by the wind?

Matthew 11:8
What then did you go out to see? A man dressed in soft clothing? Behold, those who wear soft clothing are in kings' houses.

Matthew 11:9
What then did you go out to see? A prophet? Yes, I tell you, and more than a prophet.

Matthew 11:10
This is he of whom it is written, " 'Behold, ==I send my messenger== before your face, who will prepare your way before you.'

Matthew 11:11
Truly, I say to you, among those born of women there has arisen no one greater than John the Baptist. Yet the one who is least in the <u>kingdom of heaven</u> is greater than he.

Matthew 11:12
From the days of John the Baptist until now the <u>kingdom of heaven</u> has suffered violence, and the ==violent take it by force==.

Matthew 11:13
For all the Prophets and the Law prophesied until John,

Matthew 11:14
and if you are willing to accept it, he is Elijah who is to come.

Matthew 11:15
He who has ears to hear, let him hear.

Matthew 11:16
"But to what shall I compare this generation? It is like children sitting in the marketplaces and calling to their playmates,

Matthew 11:17
" 'We played the flute for you, and you did not dance; we sang a dirge, and you did not mourn.'

Matthew 11:18
For John came neither eating nor drinking, and they say, 'He has a demon.'

Matthew 11:19
The Son of Man came eating and drinking, and they say, 'Look at him! A glutton and a drunkard, a friend of tax collectors and sinners!' Yet wisdom is justified by her deeds."

Matthew 11:21
"Woe to you, Chorazin! Woe to you, Bethsaida! For if the mighty works done in you had been done in Tyre and Sidon, they would have repented long ago in sackcloth and ashes.

Matthew 11:22
But I tell you, it will be more bearable on the day of judgment for Tyre and Sidon than for you.

Matthew 11:23
And you, Capernaum, will you be exalted to heaven? You will be brought down to Hades. For if the mighty works done in you had been done in Sodom, it would have remained until this day.

Matthew 11:24
But I tell you that it will be more tolerable on the day of judgment for the land of Sodom than for you."

Matthew 11:25
At that time Jesus declared, "I thank you, Father, Lord of heaven and earth, that you have hidden these things from the wise and understanding and revealed them to little children;

Matthew 11:26
yes, Father, for such was your gracious will.

Matthew 11:27
All things have been handed over to me by my Father, and no one knows the Son except the Father, and no one knows the Father except the Son and anyone to whom the Son chooses to reveal him.

Matthew 11:28
Come to me, all who labor and are heavy laden, and I will give you rest.

Matthew 11:29
Take my yoke upon you, and learn from me, for I am

gentle and lowly in heart, and you ==will find rest for your souls==.

Matthew 11:30
For my yoke is easy, and my burden is light."

Matthew 12:3
He said to them, "Have you not read what David did when he was hungry, and those who were with him:

Matthew 12:4
how he entered the house of God and ate the bread of the Presence, which it was not lawful for him to eat nor for those who were with him, but only for the priests?

Matthew 12:5
Or have you not read in the Law how on the Sabbath the priests in the temple profane the Sabbath and are guiltless?

Matthew 12:6
I tell you, something greater than the temple is here.

Matthew 12:7
And if you had known what this means, 'I desire mercy, and not sacrifice,' you would not have condemned the guiltless.

Matthew 12:8
For the Son of Man is lord of the Sabbath."

Matthew 12:11
He said to them, "Which one of you who has a sheep, if it falls into a pit on the Sabbath, will not take hold of it and lift it out?

Matthew 12:12
Of how much more value is a man than a sheep! So it is lawful to do good on the Sabbath."

Matthew 12:13
Then he said to the man, "Stretch out your hand." And the man stretched it out, and it was restored, healthy like the other.

Matthew 12:25
Knowing their thoughts, he said to them, "Every kingdom divided against itself is laid waste, and no city or house divided against itself will stand.

Matthew 12:26
And if Satan casts out Satan, he is divided against himself. How then will his kingdom stand?

Matthew 12:27
And if I cast out demons by Beelzebul, by whom do your sons cast them out? Therefore they will be your judges.

Matthew 12:28
But if it is by the Spirit of God that I cast out demons, then the kingdom of God has come upon you.

Matthew 12:29
Or how can someone enter a strong man's house and plunder his goods, unless he first binds the strong man? Then indeed he may plunder his house.

Matthew 12:30
Whoever is not with me is against me, and whoever does not gather with me scatters.

Matthew 12:31
Therefore I tell you, every sin and blasphemy will be forgiven people, but the blasphemy against the Spirit will not be forgiven.

Matthew 12:32
And whoever speaks a word against the Son of Man will be forgiven, but whoever speaks against the Holy Spirit will not be forgiven, either in this age or in the age to come.

Matthew 12:33
"Either make the tree good and its fruit good, or make the tree bad and its fruit bad, for the tree is known by its fruit.

Matthew 12:34
You brood of vipers! How can you speak good, when you are evil? For out of the abundance of the heart the mouth speaks.

Matthew 12:35
The good person out of his good treasure brings forth good, and the evil person out of his evil treasure brings forth evil.

Matthew 12:36
I tell you, on the day of judgment people will give account for every careless word they speak,

Matthew 12:37
for by your words you will be justified, and by your words you will be condemned."

Matthew 12:39
But he answered them, "An evil and adulterous generation seeks for a sign, but no sign will be given to it except the sign of the prophet Jonah.

Matthew 12:40
For just as Jonah was three days and three nights in the belly of the great fish, so will the Son of Man be three days and three nights in the heart of the earth.

Matthew 12:41
The men of Nineveh will rise up at the judgment with this generation and condemn it, for they repented at the preaching of Jonah, and behold, something greater than Jonah is here.

Matthew 12:42
The queen of the South will rise up at the judgment with this generation and condemn it, for she came from the ends of the earth to hear the wisdom of Solomon, and behold, something greater than Solomon is here.

Matthew 12:43
"When the unclean spirit has gone out of a person, it passes through waterless places seeking rest, but finds none.

Matthew 12:44
Then it says, 'I will return to my house from which I came.' And when it comes, it finds the house empty, swept, and put in order.

Matthew 12:45
Then it goes and brings with it seven other spirits more evil than itself, and they enter and dwell there, and the last

state of that person is worse than the first. So also will it be with this evil generation."

Matthew 12:48
But he replied to the man who told him, "Who is my mother, and who are my brothers?"

Matthew 12:49
And stretching out his hand toward his disciples, he said, "Here are my mother and my brothers!

Matthew 12:50
For whoever does the will of my Father in heaven is my brother and sister and mother."

Matthew 13:3
And he told them many things in parables, saying: "A sower went out to sow.

Matthew 13:4
And as he sowed, some seeds fell along the path, and the birds came and devoured them.

Matthew 13:5
Other seeds fell on rocky ground, where they did not have much soil, and immediately they sprang up, since they had no depth of soil,

Matthew 13:6
but when the sun rose they were scorched. And since they had no root, they withered away.

Matthew 13:7
Other seeds fell among thorns, and the thorns grew up and choked them.

Matthew 13:8
Other seeds fell on good soil and produced grain, some a hundredfold, some sixty, some thirty.

Matthew 13:9
He who has ears, let him hear."

Matthew 13:11
And he answered them, "To you it has been given to know the secrets of the kingdom of heaven, but to them it has not been given.

Matthew 13:12
For to the one who has, more will be given, and he will have an abundance, but from the one who has not, even what he has will be taken away.

Matthew 13:13
This is why I speak to them in parables, because seeing they do not see, and hearing they do not hear, nor do they understand.

Matthew 13:14
Indeed, in their case the prophecy of Isaiah is fulfilled that says: " ' "You will indeed hear but never understand, and you will indeed see but never perceive."

Matthew 13:15
For this people's heart has grown dull, and with their ears they can barely hear, and their eyes they have closed, lest they should see with their eyes and hear with their ears and understand with their heart and turn, and I would heal them.'

Matthew 13:16
But blessed are your eyes, for they see, and your ears, for they hear.

Matthew 13:17
For truly, I say to you, many prophets and righteous people longed to see what you see, and did not see it, and to hear what you hear, and did not hear it.

Matthew 13:18
"Hear then the parable of the sower:

Matthew 13:19
When anyone hears the word of the kingdom and does not understand it, the evil one comes and snatches away what has been sown in his heart. This is what was sown along the path.

Matthew 13:20
As for what was sown on rocky ground, this is the one who hears the word and immediately receives it with joy,

Matthew 13:21
yet he has no root in himself, but endures for a while, and when tribulation or persecution arises on account of the word, immediately he falls away.

Matthew 13:22
As for what was sown among thorns, this is the one who hears the word, but the cares of the world and the deceitfulness of riches choke the word, and it proves unfruitful.

Matthew 13:23
As for what was sown on good soil, this is the one who hears the word and understands it. He indeed ==bears fruit== and yields, in one case a hundredfold, in another sixty, and in another thirty."

Matthew 13:24
He put another parable before them, saying, "The **kingdom of heaven** may be compared to a man who sowed good seed in his field,

Matthew 13:25
but while his men were sleeping, his enemy came and sowed weeds among the wheat and went away.

Matthew 13:26
So when the plants came up and bore grain, then the weeds appeared also.

Matthew 13:27
And the servants of the master of the house came and said to him, 'Master, did you not sow good seed in your field? How then does it have weeds?'

Matthew 13:28
He said to them, 'An enemy has done this.' So the servants said to him, 'Then do you want us to go and gather them?'

Matthew 13:29
But he said, 'No, lest in gathering the weeds you root up the wheat along with them.

Matthew 13:30
Let both grow together until the harvest, and at harvest

time I will tell the reapers, Gather the weeds first and bind them in bundles to be burned, but gather the wheat into my barn.' "

Matthew 13:31
He put another parable before them, saying, "The kingdom of heaven is like a grain of mustard seed that a man took and sowed in his field.

Matthew 13:32
It is the smallest of all seeds, but when it has grown it is larger than all the garden plants and becomes a tree, so that the birds of the air come and make nests in its branches."

Matthew 13:33
He told them another parable. "The kingdom of heaven is like leaven that a woman took and hid in three measures of flour, till it was all leavened."

Matthew 13:37
He answered, "The one who sows the good seed is the Son of Man.

Matthew 13:38
The field is the world, and the good seed is the sons of the kingdom. The weeds are the sons of the evil one,

Matthew 13:39
and the enemy who sowed them is the devil. The harvest is the end of the age, and the reapers are angels.

Matthew 13:40
Just as the weeds are gathered and burned with fire, so will it be at the end of the age.

Matthew 13:41
The Son of Man will send his angels, and they will gather out of his kingdom all causes of sin and all law-breakers,

Matthew 13:42
and throw them into the fiery furnace. In that place there will be weeping and gnashing of teeth.

Matthew 13:43
Then the righteous will shine like the sun in the kingdom of their Father. He who has ears, let him hear.

Matthew 13:44
"The kingdom of heaven is like treasure hidden in a field, which a man found and covered up. Then in his joy he goes and sells all that he has and buys that field.

Matthew 13:45
"Again, the kingdom of heaven is like a merchant in search of fine pearls,

Matthew 13:46
who, on finding one pearl of great value, went and sold all that he had and bought it.

Matthew 13:47
"Again, the kingdom of heaven is like a net that was thrown into the sea and gathered fish of every kind.

Matthew 13:48
When it was full, men drew it ashore and sat down and sorted the good into containers but threw away the bad.

Matthew 13:49
So it will be at the end of the age. The angels will come out and separate the evil from the righteous

Matthew 13:50
and throw them into the fiery furnace. In that place there will be weeping and gnashing of teeth.

Matthew 13:51
"Have you understood all these things?" They said to him, "Yes."

Matthew 13:52
And he said to them, "Therefore every scribe who has been trained for the kingdom of heaven is like a master of a house, who brings out of his treasure what is new and what is old."

Matthew 13:57
And they took offense at him. But Jesus said to them, "A prophet is not without honor except in his hometown and in his own household."

Matthew 14:16
But Jesus said, "They need not go away; you give them something to eat."

Matthew 14:18
And he said, "Bring them here to me."

Matthew 14:27
But immediately Jesus spoke to them, saying, "Take heart; it is I. Do not be afraid."

Matthew 14:29
He said, "Come." So Peter got out of the boat and walked on the water and came to Jesus.

Matthew 14:31
Jesus immediately reached out his hand and took hold of him, saying to him, "O you of little faith, why did you doubt?"

Matthew 15:3
He answered them, "And why do you break the commandment of God for the sake of your tradition?

Matthew 15:4
For God commanded, 'Honor your father and your mother,' and, 'Whoever reviles father or mother must surely die.'

Matthew 15:5
But you say, 'If anyone tells his father or his mother, "What you would have gained from me is given to God,"

Matthew 15:6
he need not honor his father.' So for the sake of your tradition you have made void the word of God.

Matthew 15:7
You hypocrites! Well did Isaiah prophesy of you, when he said:

Matthew 15:8
" 'This people honors me with their lips, but their heart is far from me;

Matthew 15:9
in vain do they worship me, teaching as doctrines the commandments of men.' "

Matthew 15:10
And he called the people to him and said to them, "Hear and understand:

Matthew 15:11
it is not what goes into the mouth that defiles a person, but what comes out of the mouth; this defiles a person."

Matthew 15:13
He answered, "Every plant that my heavenly Father has not planted will be rooted up.

Matthew 15:14
Let them alone; they are blind guides. And if the blind lead the blind, both will fall into a pit."

Matthew 15:16
And he said, "Are you also still without understanding?

Matthew 15:17
Do you not see that whatever goes into the mouth passes into the stomach and is expelled?

Matthew 15:18
But what comes out of the mouth proceeds from the heart, and this defiles a person.

Matthew 15:19
For out of the heart come evil thoughts, murder, adultery, sexual immorality, theft, false witness, slander.

Matthew 15:20
These are what defile a person. But to eat with unwashed hands does not defile anyone."

Matthew 15:24
He answered, "I was sent only to the lost sheep of the house of Israel."

Matthew 15:26
And he answered, "It is not right to take the children's bread and throw it to the dogs."

Matthew 15:28
Then Jesus answered her, "O woman, great is your faith! Be it done for you as you desire." And her daughter was healed instantly.

Matthew 15:32
Then Jesus called his disciples to him and said, "I have compassion on the crowd because they have been with me now three days and have nothing to eat. And I am unwilling to send them away hungry, lest they faint on the way."

Matthew 15:34
And Jesus said to them, "How many loaves do you have?" They said, "Seven, and a few small fish."

Matthew 16:2
He answered them, "When it is evening, you say, 'It will be fair weather, for the sky is red.'

Matthew 16:3
And in the morning, 'It will be stormy today, for the sky is red and threatening.' You know how to interpret

the appearance of the sky, but you cannot interpret the signs of the times.

Matthew 16:4
An evil and adulterous generation seeks for a sign, but no sign will be given to it except the sign of Jonah." So he left them and departed.

Matthew 16:6
Jesus said to them, "Watch and beware of the leaven of the Pharisees and Sadducees."

Matthew 16:8
But Jesus, aware of this, said, "O you of little faith, why are you discussing among yourselves the fact that you have no bread?

Matthew 16:9
Do you not yet perceive? Do you not remember the five loaves for the five thousand, and how many baskets you gathered?

Matthew 16:10
Or the seven loaves for the four thousand, and how many baskets you gathered?

Matthew 16:11
How is it that you fail to understand that I did not speak about bread? Beware of the leaven of the Pharisees and Sadducees."

Matthew 16:13
Now when Jesus came into the district of Caesarea Philippi, he asked his disciples, "Who do people say that the Son of Man is?"

Matthew 16:15
He said to them, "But who do you say that I am?"

Matthew 16:17
And Jesus answered him, "Blessed are you, Simon Bar-Jonah! For flesh and blood has not revealed this to you, but my Father who is in heaven.

Matthew 16:18
And I tell you, you are Peter, and on this rock I will build my church, and the gates of hell shall not prevail against it.

Matthew 16:19
I will give you the keys of the kingdom of heaven, and whatever you bind on earth shall be bound in heaven, and whatever you loose on earth shall be loosed in heaven."

Matthew 16:23
But he turned and said to Peter, "Get behind me, Satan! You are a hindrance to me. For you are not setting your mind on the things of God, but on the things of man."

Matthew 16:24
Then Jesus told his disciples, "If anyone would come after me, let him deny himself and take up his cross and follow me.

Matthew 16:25
For whoever would save his life will lose it, but whoever loses his life for my sake will find it.

Matthew 16:26
For what will it profit a man if he gains the whole world

and forfeits his soul? Or what shall a man give in return for his soul?

Matthew 16:27
For the Son of Man is going to come with his angels in the glory of his Father, and then he will repay each person according to what he has done.

Matthew 16:28
Truly, I say to you, there are some standing here who will not taste death until they see the Son of Man coming in his kingdom."

Matthew 17:7
But Jesus came and touched them, saying, "Rise, and have no fear."

Matthew 17:9
And as they were coming down the mountain, Jesus commanded them, "Tell no one the vision, until the Son of Man is raised from the dead."

Matthew 17:11
He answered, "Elijah does come, and he will restore all things.

Matthew 17:12
But I tell you that Elijah has already come, and they did not recognize him, but did to him whatever they pleased. So also the Son of Man will certainly suffer at their hands."

Matthew 17:17
And Jesus answered, "O faithless and twisted generation, how long am I to be with you? How long am I to

bear with you? Bring him here to me."

Matthew 17:20
He said to them, "Because of your little faith. For truly, I say to you, if you have faith like a grain of mustard seed, you will say to this mountain, 'Move from here to there,' and it will move, and nothing will be impossible for you."

Matthew 17:22
As they were gathering in Galilee, Jesus said to them, "The Son of Man is about to be delivered into the hands of men,

Matthew 17:23
and they will kill him, and he will be raised on the third day." And they were greatly distressed.

Matthew 17:25
He said, "Yes." And when he came into the house, Jesus spoke to him first, saying, "What do you think, Simon? From whom do kings of the earth take toll or tax? From their sons or from others?"

Matthew 17:26
And when he said, "From others," Jesus said to him, "Then the sons are free.

Matthew 17:27
However, not to give offense to them, go to the sea and cast a hook and take the first fish that comes up, and when you open its mouth you will find a shekel. Take that and give it to them for me and for yourself."

Matthew 18:3
and said, "Truly, I say to you, unless you turn and become like children, you will never enter the kingdom of heaven.

Matthew 18:4
Whoever humbles himself like this child is the greatest in the kingdom of heaven.

Matthew 18:5
"Whoever receives one such child in my name receives me,

Matthew 18:6
but whoever causes one of these little ones who believe in me to sin, it would be better for him to have a great millstone fastened around his neck and to be drowned in the depth of the sea.

Matthew 18:7
"Woe to the world for temptations to sin! For it is necessary that temptations come, but woe to the one by whom the temptation comes!

Matthew 18:8
And if your hand or your foot causes you to sin, cut it off and throw it away. It is better for you to enter life crippled or lame than with two hands or two feet to be thrown into the eternal fire.

Matthew 18:9
And if your eye causes you to sin, tear it out and throw it away. It is better for you to enter life with one eye than with two eyes to be thrown into the hell of fire.

Matthew 18:10
"See that you do not despise one of these little ones. For I tell you that in heaven their angels always see the face of my Father who is in heaven.

Matthew 18:12
What do you think? If a man has a hundred sheep, and one of them has gone astray, does he not leave the ninety-nine on the mountains and go in search of the one that went astray?

Matthew 18:13
And if he finds it, truly, I say to you, he rejoices over it more than over the ninety-nine that never went astray.

Matthew 18:14
So it is not the will of my Father who is in heaven that one of these little ones should perish.

Matthew 18:15
"If your brother sins against you, go and tell him his fault, between you and him alone. If he listens to you, you have gained your brother.

Matthew 18:16
But if he does not listen, take one or two others along with you, that every charge may be established by the evidence of two or three witnesses.

Matthew 18:17
If he refuses to listen to them, tell it to the church. And if he refuses to listen even to the church, let him be to you as a Gentile and a tax collector.

Matthew 18:18
Truly, I say to you, whatever you bind on earth shall be bound in heaven, and whatever you loose on earth shall be loosed in heaven.

Matthew 18:19
Again I say to you, if two of you agree on earth about anything they ask, it will be done for them by my Father in heaven.

Matthew 18:20
For where two or three are gathered in my name, there am I among them."

Matthew 18:22
Jesus said to him, "I do not say to you seven times, but seventy-seven times.

Matthew 18:23
"Therefore the kingdom of heaven may be compared to a king who wished to settle accounts with his servants.

Matthew 18:24
When he began to settle, one was brought to him who owed him ten thousand talents.

Matthew 18:25
And since he could not pay, his master ordered him to be sold, with his wife and children and all that he had, and payment to be made.

Matthew 18:26
So the servant fell on his knees, imploring him, 'Have patience with me, and I will pay you everything.'

Matthew 18:27
And out of pity for him, the master of that servant released him and forgave him the debt.

Matthew 18:28
But when that same servant went out, he found one of his fellow servants who owed him a hundred denarii, and seizing him, he began to choke him, saying, 'Pay what you owe.'

Matthew 18:29
So his fellow servant fell down and pleaded with him, 'Have patience with me, and I will pay you.'

Matthew 18:30
He refused and went and put him in prison until he should pay the debt.

Matthew 18:31
When his fellow servants saw what had taken place, they were greatly distressed, and they went and reported to their master all that had taken place.

Matthew 18:32
Then his master summoned him and said to him, 'You wicked servant! I forgave you all that debt because you pleaded with me.

Matthew 18:33
And should not you have had mercy on your fellow servant, as I had mercy on you?'

Matthew 18:34
And in anger his master delivered him to the jailers, until he should pay all his debt.

Matthew 18:35
So also my heavenly Father will do to every one of you, if you do not forgive your brother from your heart."

Matthew 19:4
He answered, "Have you not read that he who created them from the beginning made them male and female,

Matthew 19:5
and said, 'Therefore a man shall leave his father and his mother and hold fast to his wife, and the two shall become one flesh'?

Matthew 19:6
So they are no longer two but one flesh. What therefore God has joined together, let not man separate."

Matthew 19:8
He said to them, "Because of your hardness of heart Moses allowed you to divorce your wives, but from the beginning it was not so.

Matthew 19:9
And I say to you: whoever divorces his wife, except for sexual immorality, and marries another, commits adultery."

Matthew 19:11
But he said to them, "Not everyone can receive this saying, but only those to whom it is given.

Matthew 19:12
For there are eunuchs who have been so from birth, and there are eunuchs who have been made eunuchs by

men, and there are eunuchs who have made themselves eunuchs for the sake of the kingdom of heaven. Let the one who is able to receive this receive it."

Matthew 19:14
but Jesus said, "Let the little children come to me and do not hinder them, for to such belongs the kingdom of heaven."

Matthew 19:17
And he said to him, "Why do you ask me about what is good? There is only one who is good. If you would enter life, keep the commandments."

Matthew 19:18
He said to him, "Which ones?" And Jesus said, "You shall not murder, You shall not commit adultery, You shall not steal, You shall not bear false witness,

Matthew 19:19
Honor your father and mother, and, You shall love your neighbor as yourself."

Matthew 19:21
Jesus said to him, "If you would be perfect, go, sell what you possess and give to the poor, and you will have treasure in heaven; and come, follow me."

Matthew 19:23
And Jesus said to his disciples, "Truly, I say to you, only with difficulty will a rich person enter the kingdom of heaven.

Matthew 19:24
Again I tell you, it is easier for a camel to go through

the eye of a needle than for a rich person to enter the kingdom of God."

Matthew 19:26
But Jesus looked at them and said, "With man this is impossible, but with God all things are possible."

Matthew 19:28
Jesus said to them, "Truly, I say to you, in the new world, when the Son of Man will sit on his glorious throne, you who have followed me will also sit on twelve thrones, judging the twelve tribes of Israel.

Matthew 19:29
And everyone who has left houses or brothers or sisters or father or mother or children or lands, for my name's sake, will receive a hundredfold and will inherit eternal life.

Matthew 19:30
But many who are first will be last, and the last first.

Matthew 20:1
"For the kingdom of heaven is like a master of a house who went out early in the morning to hire laborers for his vineyard.

Matthew 20:2
After agreeing with the laborers for a denarius a day, he sent them into his vineyard.

Matthew 20:3
And going out about the third hour he saw others standing idle in the marketplace,

Matthew 20:4
and to them he said, 'You go into the vineyard too, and whatever is right I will give you.'

Matthew 20:5
So they went. Going out again about the sixth hour and the ninth hour, he did the same.

Matthew 20:6
And about the eleventh hour he went out and found others standing. And he said to them, 'Why do you stand here idle all day?'

Matthew 20:7
They said to him, 'Because no one has hired us.' He said to them, 'You go into the vineyard too.'

Matthew 20:8
And when evening came, the owner of the vineyard said to his foreman, 'Call the laborers and pay them their wages, beginning with the last, up to the first.'

Matthew 20:9
And when those hired about the eleventh hour came, each of them received a denarius.

Matthew 20:10
Now when those hired first came, they thought they would receive more, but each of them also received a denarius.

Matthew 20:11
And on receiving it they grumbled at the master of the house,

Matthew 20:12
saying, 'These last worked only one hour, and you have made them equal to us who have borne the burden of the day and the scorching heat.'

Matthew 20:13
But he replied to one of them, 'Friend, I am doing you no wrong. Did you not agree with me for a denarius?

Matthew 20:14
Take what belongs to you and go. I choose to give to this last worker as I give to you.

Matthew 20:15
Am I not allowed to do what I choose with what belongs to me? Or do you begrudge my generosity?'

Matthew 20:16
So the last will be first, and the first last."

Matthew 20:18
"See, we are going up to Jerusalem. And the Son of Man will be delivered over to the chief priests and scribes, and they will condemn him to death

Matthew 20:19
and deliver him over to the Gentiles to be mocked and flogged and crucified, and he will be raised on the third day."

Matthew 20:21
And he said to her, "What do you want?" She said to him, "Say that these two sons of mine are to sit, one at your right hand and one at your left, in your kingdom."

Matthew 20:22
Jesus answered, "You do not know what you are asking. Are you able to drink the cup that I am to drink?" They said to him, "We are able."

Matthew 20:23
He said to them, "You will drink my cup, but to sit at my right hand and at my left is not mine to grant, but it is for those for whom it has been prepared by my Father."

Matthew 20:25
But Jesus called them to him and said, "You know that the rulers of the Gentiles lord it over them, and their great ones exercise authority over them.

Matthew 20:26
It shall not be so among you. But whoever would be great among you must be your servant,

Matthew 20:27
and whoever would be first among you must be your slave,

Matthew 20:28
even as the Son of Man came not to be served but to serve, and to give his life as a ransom for many."

Matthew 20:32
And stopping, Jesus called them and said, "What do you want me to do for you?"

Matthew 21:2
saying to them, "Go into the village in front of you, and immediately you will find a donkey tied, and a colt with her. Untie them and bring them to me.

Matthew 21:3
If anyone says anything to you, you shall say, 'The Lord needs them,' and he will send them at once."

Matthew 21:13
He said to them, "It is written, 'My house shall be called a house of prayer,' but you make it a den of robbers."

Matthew 21:16
and they said to him, "Do you hear what these are saying?" And Jesus said to them, "Yes; have you never read, " 'Out of the mouth of infants and nursing babies you have prepared praise'?"

Matthew 21:19
And seeing a fig tree by the wayside, he went to it and found nothing on it but only leaves. And he said to it, "May no fruit ever come from you again!" And the fig tree withered at once.

Matthew 21:21
And Jesus answered them, "Truly, I say to you, if you have faith and do not doubt, you will not only do what has been done to the fig tree, but even if you say to this mountain, 'Be taken up and thrown into the sea,' it will happen.

Matthew 21:22
And whatever you ask in prayer, you will receive, if you have faith."

Matthew 21:24
Jesus answered them, "I also will ask you one question, and if you tell me the answer, then I also will tell you by what authority I do these things.

Matthew 21:25
The baptism of John, from where did it come? From heaven or from man?" And they discussed it among themselves, saying, "If we say, 'From heaven,' he will say to us, 'Why then did you not believe him?'

Matthew 21:27
So they answered Jesus, "We do not know." And he said to them, "Neither will I tell you by what authority I do these things.

Matthew 21:28
"What do you think? A man had two sons. And he went to the first and said, 'Son, go and work in the vineyard today.'

Matthew 21:29
And he answered, 'I will not,' but afterward he changed his mind and went.

Matthew 21:30
And he went to the other son and said the same. And he answered, 'I go, sir,' but did not go.

Matthew 21:31
Which of the two did the will of his father?" They said, "The first." Jesus said to them, "Truly, I say to you, the tax collectors and the prostitutes go into the kingdom of God before you.

Matthew 21:32
For John came to you in the way of righteousness, and you did not believe him, but the tax collectors and the prostitutes believed him. And even when you saw it, you did not afterward change your minds and believe him.

Matthew 21:33
"Hear another parable. There was a master of a house who planted a vineyard and put a fence around it and dug a winepress in it and built a tower and leased it to tenants, and went into another country.

Matthew 21:34
When the season for fruit drew near, he sent his servants to the tenants to get his fruit.

Matthew 21:35
And the tenants took his servants and beat one, killed another, and stoned another.

Matthew 21:36
Again he sent other servants, more than the first. And they did the same to them.

Matthew 21:37
Finally he sent his son to them, saying, 'They will respect my son.'

Matthew 21:38
But when the tenants saw the son, they said to themselves, 'This is the heir. Come, let us kill him and have his inheritance.'

Matthew 21:39
And they took him and threw him out of the vineyard and killed him.

Matthew 21:40
When therefore the owner of the vineyard comes, what will he do to those tenants?"

Matthew 21:42
Jesus said to them, "Have you never read in the Scriptures: " 'The stone that the builders rejected has become the cornerstone; this was the Lord's doing, and it is marvelous in our eyes'?

Matthew 21:43
Therefore I tell you, the kingdom of God will be taken away from you and given to a people producing its fruits.

Matthew 21:44
And the one who falls on this stone will be broken to pieces; and when it falls on anyone, it will crush him."

Matthew 22:2
"The kingdom of heaven may be compared to a king who gave a wedding feast for his son,

Matthew 22:3
and sent his servants to call those who were invited to the wedding feast, but they would not come.

Matthew 22:4
Again he sent other servants, saying, 'Tell those who are invited, "See, I have prepared my dinner, my oxen and my fat calves have been slaughtered, and everything is ready. Come to the wedding feast." '

Matthew 22:5
But they paid no attention and went off, one to his farm, another to his business,

Matthew 22:6
while the rest seized his servants, treated them shame-

fully, and killed them.

Matthew 22:7
The king was angry, and he sent his troops and destroyed those murderers and burned their city.

Matthew 22:8
Then he said to his servants, 'The wedding feast is ready, but those invited were not worthy.

Matthew 22:9
Go therefore to the main roads and invite to the wedding feast as many as you find.'

Matthew 22:10
And those servants went out into the roads and gathered all whom they found, both bad and good. So the wedding hall was filled with guests.

Matthew 22:11
"But when the king came in to look at the guests, he saw there a man who had no wedding garment.

Matthew 22:12
And he said to him, 'Friend, how did you get in here without a wedding garment?' And he was speechless.

Matthew 22:13
Then the king said to the attendants, 'Bind him hand and foot and cast him into the outer darkness. In that place there will be weeping and gnashing of teeth.'

Matthew 22:14
For many are called, but few are chosen."

Matthew 22:18
But Jesus, aware of their malice, said, "Why put me to the test, you hypocrites?

Matthew 22:19
Show me the coin for the tax." And they brought him a denarius.

Matthew 22:20
And Jesus said to them, "Whose likeness and inscription is this?"

Matthew 22:21
They said, "Caesar's." Then he said to them, "Therefore render to Caesar the things that are Caesar's, and to God the things that are God's."

Matthew 22:29
But Jesus answered them, "You are wrong, because you know neither the Scriptures nor the power of God.

Matthew 22:30
For in the resurrection they neither marry nor are given in marriage, but are like angels in heaven.

Matthew 22:31
And as for the resurrection of the dead, have you not read what was said to you by God:

Matthew 22:32
'I am the God of Abraham, and the God of Isaac, and the God of Jacob'? He is not God of the dead, but of the living."

Matthew 22:37
And he said to him, "You shall love the Lord your God with all your heart and with all your soul and with all your mind.

Matthew 22:38
This is the great and first commandment.

Matthew 22:39
And a second is like it: You shall love your neighbor as yourself.

Matthew 22:40
On these two commandments depend all the Law and the Prophets."

Matthew 22:42
saying, "What do you think about the Christ? Whose son is he?" They said to him, "The son of David."

Matthew 22:43
He said to them, "How is it then that David, in the Spirit, calls him Lord, saying,

Matthew 22:44
" 'The Lord said to my Lord, "Sit at my right hand, until I put your enemies under your feet" '?

Matthew 22:45
If then David calls him Lord, how is he his son?"

Matthew 23:2
"The scribes and the Pharisees sit on Moses' seat,

Matthew 23:3
so do and observe whatever they tell you, but not the works they do. For they preach, but do not practice.

Matthew 23:4
They tie up heavy burdens, hard to bear, and lay them on people's shoulders, but they themselves are not willing to move them with their finger.

Matthew 23:5
They do all their deeds to be seen by others. For they make their phylacteries broad and their fringes long,

Matthew 23:6
and they love the place of honor at feasts and the best seats in the synagogues

Matthew 23:7
and greetings in the marketplaces and being called rabbi by others.

Matthew 23:8
But you are not to be called rabbi, for you have one teacher, and you are all brothers.

Matthew 23:9
And call no man your father on earth, for you have one Father, who is in heaven.

Matthew 23:10
Neither be called instructors, for you have one instructor, the Christ.

Matthew 23:11
The greatest among you shall be your servant.

Matthew 23:12
Whoever exalts himself will be humbled, and whoever humbles himself will be exalted.

Matthew 23:13
"But woe to you, scribes and Pharisees, hypocrites! For you shut the kingdom of heaven in people's faces. For you neither enter yourselves nor allow those who would enter to go in.

Matthew 23:15
Woe to you, scribes and Pharisees, hypocrites! For you travel across sea and land to make a single proselyte, and when he becomes a proselyte, you make him twice as much a child of hell as yourselves.

Matthew 23:16
"Woe to you, blind guides, who say, 'If anyone swears by the temple, it is nothing, but if anyone swears by the gold of the temple, he is bound by his oath.'

Matthew 23:17
You blind fools! For which is greater, the gold or the temple that has made the gold sacred?

Matthew 23:18
And you say, 'If anyone swears by the altar, it is nothing, but if anyone swears by the gift that is on the altar, he is bound by his oath.'

Matthew 23:19
You blind men! For which is greater, the gift or the altar that makes the gift sacred?

Matthew 23:20
So whoever swears by the altar swears by it and by everything on it.

Matthew 23:21
And whoever swears by the temple swears by it and by him who dwells in it.

Matthew 23:22
And whoever swears by heaven swears by the throne of God and by him who sits upon it.

Matthew 23:23
"Woe to you, scribes and Pharisees, hypocrites! For you tithe mint and dill and cumin, and have neglected the weightier matters of the law: justice and mercy and faithfulness. These you ought to have done, without neglecting the others.

Matthew 23:24
You blind guides, straining out a gnat and swallowing a camel!

Matthew 23:25
"Woe to you, scribes and Pharisees, hypocrites! For you clean the outside of the cup and the plate, but inside they are full of greed and self-indulgence.

Matthew 23:26
You blind Pharisee! First clean the inside of the cup and the plate, that the outside also may be clean.

Matthew 23:27
"Woe to you, scribes and Pharisees, hypocrites! For you are like whitewashed tombs, which outwardly appear

beautiful, but within are full of dead people's bones and all uncleanness.

Matthew 23:28
So you also outwardly appear righteous to others, but within you are full of hypocrisy and lawlessness.

Matthew 23:29
"Woe to you, scribes and Pharisees, hypocrites! For you build the tombs of the prophets and decorate the monuments of the righteous,

Matthew 23:30
saying, 'If we had lived in the days of our fathers, we would not have taken part with them in shedding the blood of the prophets.'

Matthew 23:31
Thus you witness against yourselves that you are sons of those who murdered the prophets.

Matthew 23:32
Fill up, then, the measure of your fathers.

Matthew 23:33
You serpents, you brood of vipers, how are you to escape being sentenced to hell?

Matthew 23:34
Therefore I send you prophets and wise men and scribes, some of whom you will kill and crucify, and some you will flog in your synagogues and persecute from town to town,

Matthew 23:35
so that on you may come all the righteous blood shed on earth, from the blood of righteous Abel to the blood of Zechariah the son of Barachiah, whom you murdered between the sanctuary and the altar.

Matthew 23:36
Truly, I say to you, all these things will come upon this generation.

Matthew 23:37
"O Jerusalem, Jerusalem, the city that kills the prophets and stones those who are sent to it! How often would I have gathered your children together as a hen gathers her brood under her wings, and you were not willing!

Matthew 23:38
See, your house is left to you desolate.

Matthew 23:39
For I tell you, you will not see me again, until you say, 'Blessed is he who comes in the name of the Lord.' "

Matthew 24:2
But he answered them, "You see all these, do you not? Truly, I say to you, there will not be left here one stone upon another that will not be thrown down."

Matthew 24:4
And Jesus answered them, "See that no one leads you astray.

Matthew 24:5
For many will come in my name, saying, 'I am the Christ,' and they will lead many astray.

Matthew 24:6
And you will hear of wars and rumors of wars. See that you are not alarmed, for this must take place, but the end is not yet.

Matthew 24:7
For nation will rise against nation, and kingdom against kingdom, and there will be famines and earthquakes in various places.

Matthew 24:8
All these are but the beginning of the birth pains.

Matthew 24:9
"Then they will deliver you up to tribulation and put you to death, and you will be hated by all nations for my name's sake.

Matthew 24:10
And then many will fall away and betray one another and hate one another.

Matthew 24:11
And many false prophets will arise and lead many astray.

Matthew 24:12
And because lawlessness will be increased, the love of many will grow cold.

Matthew 24:13
But the one who endures to the end will be saved.

Matthew 24:14
And this gospel of the kingdom will be proclaimed

throughout the whole world as a testimony to all nations, and then the end will come.

Matthew 24:15
"So when you see the abomination of desolation spoken of by the prophet Daniel, standing in the holy place (let the reader understand),

Matthew 24:16
then let those who are in Judea flee to the mountains.

Matthew 24:17
Let the one who is on the housetop not go down to take what is in his house,

Matthew 24:18
and let the one who is in the field not turn back to take his cloak.

Matthew 24:19
And alas for women who are pregnant and for those who are nursing infants in those days!

Matthew 24:20
Pray that your flight may not be in winter or on a Sabbath.

Matthew 24:21
For then there will be great tribulation, such as has not been from the beginning of the world until now, no, and never will be.

Matthew 24:22
And if those days had not been cut short, no human being would be saved. But for the sake of the elect those

days will be cut short.

Matthew 24:23
Then if anyone says to you, 'Look, here is the Christ!' or 'There he is!' do not believe it.

Matthew 24:24
For false christs and false prophets will arise and perform great signs and wonders, so as to lead astray, if possible, even the elect.

Matthew 24:25
See, I have told you beforehand.

Matthew 24:26
So, if they say to you, 'Look, he is in the wilderness,' do not go out. If they say, 'Look, he is in the inner rooms,' do not believe it.

Matthew 24:27
For as the lightning comes from the east and shines as far as the west, so will be the coming of the Son of Man.

Matthew 24:28
Wherever the corpse is, there the vultures will gather.

Matthew 24:29
"Immediately after the tribulation of those days the sun will be darkened, and the moon will not give its light, and the stars will fall from heaven, and the powers of the heavens will be shaken.

Matthew 24:30
Then will appear in heaven the sign of the Son of Man, and then all the tribes of the earth will mourn, and they

will see the Son of Man coming on the clouds of heaven with power and great glory.

Matthew 24:31
And he will send out his angels with a loud trumpet call, and they will gather his elect from the four winds, from one end of heaven to the other.

Matthew 24:32
"From the fig tree learn its lesson: as soon as its branch becomes tender and puts out its leaves, you know that summer is near.

Matthew 24:33
So also, when you see all these things, you know that he is near, at the very gates.

Matthew 24:34
Truly, I say to you, this generation will not pass away until all these things take place.

Matthew 24:35
Heaven and earth will pass away, but my words will not pass away.

Matthew 24:36
"But concerning that day and hour no one knows, not even the angels of heaven, nor the Son, but the Father only.

Matthew 24:37
For as were the days of Noah, so will be the coming of the Son of Man.

Matthew 24:38
For as in those days before the flood they were eating and drinking, marrying and giving in marriage, until the day when Noah entered the ark,

Matthew 24:39
and they were unaware until the flood came and swept them all away, so will be the coming of the Son of Man.

Matthew 24:40
Then two men will be in the field; one will be taken and one left.

Matthew 24:41
Two women will be grinding at the mill; one will be taken and one left.

Matthew 24:42
Therefore, ==stay awake==, for you do not know on what day your Lord is coming.

Matthew 24:43
But ==know this==, that if the master of the house had known in what part of the night the thief was coming, he would have stayed awake and would not have let his house be broken into.

Matthew 24:44
Therefore you also ==must be ready==, for the Son of Man is coming at an hour you do not expect.

Matthew 24:45
"Who then is the faithful and wise servant, whom his master has set over his household, to give them their food at the proper time?

Matthew 24:46
Blessed is that servant whom his master will find ==so doing== when he comes.

Matthew 24:47
Truly, I say to you, he will set him over all his possessions.

Matthew 24:48
But if that wicked servant says to himself, 'My master is delayed,'

Matthew 24:49
and begins to ~~beat his fellow servants~~ and ~~eats and drinks~~ with drunkards,

Matthew 24:50
the master of that servant will come on a day when he does not expect him and at an hour he does not know

Matthew 24:51
and will cut him in pieces and put him with the hypocrites. In that place there will be weeping and gnashing of teeth.

Matthew 25:1
"Then the ==kingdom of heaven== will be like ten virgins who took their lamps and went to meet the bridegroom.

Matthew 25:2
Five of them were foolish, and five were wise.

Matthew 25:3
For when the foolish took their lamps, they took no oil with them,

Matthew 25:4
but the wise took flasks of oil with their lamps.

Matthew 25:5
As the bridegroom was delayed, they all became drowsy and slept.

Matthew 25:6
But at midnight there was a cry, 'Here is the bridegroom! Come out to meet him.'

Matthew 25:7
Then all those virgins rose and trimmed their lamps.

Matthew 25:8
And the foolish said to the wise, 'Give us some of your oil, for our lamps are going out.'

Matthew 25:9
But the wise answered, saying, 'Since there will not be enough for us and for you, go rather to the dealers and buy for yourselves.'

Matthew 25:10
And while they were going to buy, the bridegroom came, and those who were ready went in with him to the marriage feast, and the door was shut.

Matthew 25:11
Afterward the other virgins came also, saying, 'Lord, lord, open to us.'

Matthew 25:12
But he answered, 'Truly, I say to you, I do not know you.'

Matthew 25:13
Watch therefore, for you know neither the day nor the hour.

Matthew 25:14
"For it will be like a man going on a journey, who called his servants and entrusted to them his property.

Matthew 25:15
To one he gave five talents, to another two, to another one, to each according to his ability. Then he went away.

Matthew 25:16
He who had received the five talents went at once and traded with them, and he made five talents more.

Matthew 25:17
So also he who had the two talents made two talents more.

Matthew 25:18
But he who had received the one talent went and dug in the ground and hid his master's money.

Matthew 25:19
Now after a long time the master of those servants came and settled accounts with them.

Matthew 25:20
And he who had received the five talents came forward, bringing five talents more, saying, 'Master, you delivered to me five talents; here I have made five talents more.'

Matthew 25:21
His master said to him, 'Well done, good and faithful servant. You have been faithful over a little; I will set you over much. Enter into the joy of your master.'

Matthew 25:22
And he also who had the two talents came forward, saying, 'Master, you delivered to me two talents; here I have made two talents more.'

Matthew 25:23
His master said to him, 'Well done, good and faithful servant. You have been faithful over a little; I will set you over much. Enter into the joy of your master.'

Matthew 25:24
He also who had received the one talent came forward, saying, 'Master, I knew you to be a hard man, reaping where you did not sow, and gathering where you scattered no seed,

Matthew 25:25
so I was afraid, and I went and hid your talent in the ground. Here you have what is yours.'

Matthew 25:26
But his master answered him, 'You wicked and slothful servant! You knew that I reap where I have not sown and gather where I scattered no seed?

Matthew 25:27
Then you ought to have invested my money with the bankers, and at my coming I should have received what was my own with interest.

Matthew 25:28
So take the talent from him and give it to him who has the ten talents.

Matthew 25:29
For to everyone who has will more be given, and he will have an abundance. But from the one who has not, even what he has will be taken away.

Matthew 25:30
And cast the worthless servant into the outer darkness. In that place there will be weeping and gnashing of teeth.'

Matthew 25:31
"When the Son of Man comes in his glory, and all the angels with him, then he will sit on his glorious throne.

Matthew 25:32
Before him will be gathered all the nations, and he will separate people one from another as a shepherd separates the sheep from the goats.

Matthew 25:33
And he will place the sheep on his right, but the goats on the left.

Matthew 25:34
Then the King will say to those on his right, 'Come, you who are blessed by my Father, inherit the kingdom prepared for you from the foundation of the world.

Matthew 25:35
For I was hungry and you gave me food, I was thirsty

and you gave me drink, I was a stranger and you welcomed me,

Matthew 25:36
I was naked and you clothed me, I was sick and you visited me, I was in prison and you came to me.'

Matthew 25:37
Then the righteous will answer him, saying, 'Lord, when did we see you hungry and feed you, or thirsty and give you drink?

Matthew 25:38
And when did we see you a stranger and welcome you, or naked and clothe you?

Matthew 25:39
And when did we see you sick or in prison and visit you?'

Matthew 25:40
And the King will answer them, 'Truly, I say to you, as you did it to one of the least of these my brothers, you did it to me.'

Matthew 25:41
"Then he will say to those on his left, 'Depart from me, you cursed, into the eternal fire prepared for the devil and his angels.

Matthew 25:42
For I was hungry and you gave me no food, I was thirsty and you gave me no drink,

Matthew 25:43
I was a stranger and ~~you did not welcome me~~, naked and ~~you did not clothe me~~, sick and in prison and ~~you did not visit me~~.'

Matthew 25:44
Then they also will answer, saying, 'Lord, when did we see you hungry or thirsty or a stranger or naked or sick or in prison, and did not minister to you?'

Matthew 25:45
Then he will answer them, saying, 'Truly, I say to you, as ~~you did not do it to one of the least of these, you did not do it to me~~.'

Matthew 25:46
And these will go away into eternal punishment, but the righteous into eternal life."

Matthew 26:2
"You know that after two days the Passover is coming, and the Son of Man will be delivered up to be crucified."

Matthew 26:10
But Jesus, aware of this, said to them, "Why do you trouble the woman? For she has done a beautiful thing to me.

Matthew 26:11
For you always have the poor with you, but you will not always have me.

Matthew 26:12
In pouring this ointment on my body, she has done it to prepare me for burial.

Matthew 26:13
Truly, I say to you, wherever this gospel is proclaimed in the whole world, what she has done will also be told in memory of her."

Matthew 26:18
He said, "Go into the city to a certain man and say to him, 'The Teacher says, My time is at hand. I will keep the Passover at your house with my disciples.' "

Matthew 26:21
And as they were eating, he said, "Truly, I say to you, one of you will betray me."

Matthew 26:23
He answered, "He who has dipped his hand in the dish with me will betray me.

Matthew 26:24
The Son of Man goes as it is written of him, but woe to that man by whom the Son of Man is betrayed! It would have been better for that man if he had not been born."

Matthew 26:25
Judas, who would betray him, answered, "Is it I, Rabbi?" He said to him, "You have said so."

Matthew 26:26
Now as they were eating, Jesus took bread, and after blessing it broke it and gave it to the disciples, and said, "Take, eat; this is my body."

Matthew 26:27
And he took a cup, and when he had given thanks he gave it to them, saying, "Drink of it, all of you,

Matthew 26:28
for this is my blood of the covenant, which is poured out for many for the forgiveness of sins.

Matthew 26:29
I tell you I will not drink again of this fruit of the vine until that day when I drink it new with you in my Father's kingdom."

Matthew 26:31
Then Jesus said to them, "You will all fall away because of me this night. For it is written, 'I will strike the shepherd, and the sheep of the flock will be scattered.'

Matthew 26:32
But after I am raised up, I will go before you to Galilee."

Matthew 26:34
Jesus said to him, "Truly, I tell you, this very night, before the rooster crows, you will deny me three times."

Matthew 26:36
Then Jesus went with them to a place called Gethsemane, and he said to his disciples, "Sit here, while I go over there and pray."

Matthew 26:38
Then he said to them, "My soul is very sorrowful, even to death; remain here, and watch with me."

Matthew 26:39
And going a little farther he fell on his face and prayed, saying, "My Father, if it be possible, let this cup pass from me; nevertheless, not as I will, but as you will."

Matthew 26:40
And he came to the disciples and found them sleeping. And he said to Peter, "So, could you not watch with me one hour?

Matthew 26:41
Watch and pray that you may not enter into temptation. The spirit indeed is willing, but the flesh is weak."

Matthew 26:42
Again, for the second time, he went away and prayed, "My Father, if this cannot pass unless I drink it, your will be done."

Matthew 26:45
Then he came to the disciples and said to them, "Sleep and take your rest later on. See, the hour is at hand, and the Son of Man is betrayed into the hands of sinners.

Matthew 26:46
Rise, let us be going; see, my betrayer is at hand."

Matthew 26:50
Jesus said to him, "Friend, do what you came to do." Then they came up and laid hands on Jesus and seized him.

Matthew 26:52
Then Jesus said to him, "Put your sword back into its place. For all who take the sword will perish by the sword.

Matthew 26:53
Do you think that I cannot appeal to my Father, and he

will at once send me more than twelve legions of angels?

Matthew 26:54
But how then should the Scriptures be fulfilled, that it must be so?"

Matthew 26:55
At that hour Jesus said to the crowds, "Have you come out as against a robber, with swords and clubs to capture me? Day after day I sat in the temple teaching, and you did not seize me.

Matthew 26:56
But all this has taken place that the Scriptures of the prophets might be fulfilled." Then all the disciples left him and fled.

Matthew 26:64
Jesus said to him, "You have said so. But I tell you, from now on you will see the Son of Man seated at the right hand of Power and coming on the clouds of heaven."

Matthew 26:75
And Peter remembered the saying of Jesus, "Before the rooster crows, you will deny me three times." And he went out and wept bitterly.

Matthew 27:11
Now Jesus stood before the governor, and the governor asked him, "Are you the King of the Jews?" Jesus said, "You have said so."

Matthew 27:46
And about the ninth hour Jesus cried out with a loud voice, saying, "Eli, Eli, lema sabachthani?" that is, "My

God, my God, why have you forsaken me?"

Matthew 28:9
And behold, Jesus met them and said, "Greetings!" And they came up and took hold of his feet and worshiped him.

Matthew 28:10
Then Jesus said to them, "Do not be afraid; go and tell my brothers to go to Galilee, and there they will see me."

Matthew 28:18
And Jesus came and said to them, "All authority in heaven and on earth has been given to me.

Matthew 28:19
Go therefore and make disciples of all nations, baptizing them in the name of the Father and of the Son and of the Holy Spirit,

Matthew 28:20
teaching them to observe all that I have commanded you. And behold, I am with you always, to the end of the age."

choose

choose believe
choose to believe the Truth
choose to leave behind all the lies
choose to believe your identity
choose to live life abundantly

"The thief comes only in order to steal and kill and destroy. I came that they may have and enjoy life, and have it in abundance [to the full, till it overflows]." - Jesus

CPSIA information can be obtained
at www.ICGtesting.com
Printed in the USA
BVHW02s2330151018
530228BV00033B/1148/P

9 781388 704193